THE WAR AGAINST THE LUFTWAFFE 1943-1944

THE UNTOLD STORY OF THE AIR WAR AGAINST GERMANY AND HOW WORLD WAR II HUNG IN THE BALANCE

L. DOUGLAS KEENEY

PUBLISHED BY FASTPENCIL, INC.

Contents

FOREWORD

From the remove of the 21st Century it would seem quite unlikely that an agreement to target Adolf Hitler's Nazi Germany with the full force of Great Britain and the United States came about only after negotiation between the two allies and, even then, as late as the start of 1943, but it did. On January 21, 1943, the combined Joint Chiefs of Staff for the British and American military forces signed the defining military document that spelled out the plan to defeat Nazi Germany. The Casablanca Directive, as it was known, called for a multinational military campaign of utmost violence against Nazi Germany to bring about "the progressive destruction and dislocation of the German military, industrial, and economic system, and the undermining of the morale of the German people to a point where their capacity for armed resistance is fatally weakened." Key to this directive was the phrase "fatally weakened." Surrender, President Franklin Roosevelt would later announce, would not be negotiated.

Out of the Casablanca Directive came the air war plan. The British Royal Air Force and U.S. Army Air Forces agreed to what was called the Combined Bomber Offensive (CBO). The British would bomb German cities by night; the Americans would bomb German factories and airfields by day.

Within the CBO was a list of over 30,000 targets that included tank factories, munitions depots, army bases, radar sites, control facilities, airframe factories, oil refineries, transportation hubs, ammunition factories, electrical grids, and other key infrastructure elements. However, inside the CBO was a war plan-within-a-war plan that specifically targeted the German Air Force (GAF). This was called Pointblank. Pointblank was designed to eliminate the Luftwaffe as a force in being. Said one British planner: "If the growth of the German fighter strength is not arrested quickly, it may become literally impossible to carry out the destruction planned,m which would create the conditions necessary for ultimate decisive action by our combined forces on the continent."

Pointblank would become one of the most difficult, deadliest, time-consuming and destructive battles of World War II. To have any chance at all, bombers had to go deep into the heart of Germany against heavily defended manufacturing companies with well-known names such as Messerschmitt, Focke-Wulf, Dornier, Junkers, and Heinkel. The very best that America had would be pitted against the battle-hardened German Air Force with their formidable combination of radar, air interceptors and ground based anti-aircraft artillery. Tactics would be cut from whole cloth; missions would teach lessons written in blood. Air battles would be fought with intense savagery, and losses on both sides would be staggering. On some missions, fifty to seventy per cent of attacking German fighters would be shoot down. On the American side, losses of 600 airmen would be a frightful reality and not at all uncommon. Said one airman in his memoirs: "When the Germans attacked, they would cut in and out of us, shooting at whatever there was. You could see hundreds of flak shells exploding all around you. Men were bailing out of burning bombers and landing on the craft underneath them. It was horrible."

The flak made it even worse. "We lost two B-17s to flak that day," wrote a Mississippi airman in a history of air crews from that state. "I think, in heavy flak like that, any one of us would have just as soon have turned around and gone home. But there were 10,000 of us up there at 28,000 feet over the city, and we had a great tradition: we never once turned back in the face of enemy action."

By the fall of 1943, success seemed elusive. The Germans seemed no less capable of killing now than they had months before when bombing swung into action. German engineers, known for their precision and redundancy, had fine-tuned their military-industrial complex and it was surviving the bombs. More fighters were coming off the production lines now than a year ago — and record numbers would come off in the months ahead. Clearly something was wrong with Pointblank

On January 1, 1944, General Henry H. "Hap" Arnold, commander of the United States Army Air Forces, reorganized his command in Europe by putting his lifelong friend General Carl A. "Tooey" Spaatz in command of the strategic bombing forces in England and Italy, and his protégé, General James "Jimmy" Doolittle in command of the Eight Air Force in England. Said Arnold to his new commanders: "Give me air superiority over the D-Day beaches."

Tooey Spaatz moved to England, settling into a Victorian mansion on the edge of Bushy Park in Wimbledon Common just up the Thames from London. Jimmy Doolittle's headquarters was not far away, located in a fifteen room home rented from a retired British couple on the Thames. Doolittle was an immediate hit with the men. "He had just the right mix," said one of his pilots at a forward bomber base. "He was a forceful leader and approachable as a man." On his first day of duty, Doolittle issued an order that made his intentions clear. "If it moved, could fly, or supported the German war effort," said Doolittle in his memoir, "I told my pilots to kill it in place." On a wall in one of the briefing rooms Doolittle replaced a sign that said that the first duty of the Eighth Air Force fighters was to get the bombers back safely. The new sign would say: "The First Duty of the Eighth Air Force Fighters is to Destroy German Fighters."

On January 9, 1944, Spaatz and Doolittle mounted their first major raid, only to see sixty of their bombers shot down at a loss of 600 men. Surviving B-17s, crippled by the murderous fire, limped home with bloodied cabins and gravely wounded men. "They had their very best pilots in the air against us that day," remembered a somber pilot as recounted in a history of the air war. A worried Hap Arnold wrote his British counterpart, Air Marshal Sir Charles Portal. "The planned invasion hangs directly on the success of our combined aerial offensive," said Arnold. "I am sure our failure to decisively cripple both the sources of German air power and the GAF itself is causing you and me real concern."

On February 19, 1944, the tide began to turn. After a month of bad weather there was a slight opening, perhaps enough to start hitting the Germans with the intensity of hundreds of B-17s. On that day, more than 1,600 bombers and fighters were fueled, bombed-up and ready to go. Spaatz called Doolittle for a weather report. Doolittle reported marginal conditions with the prospect of icing, not good for flying but not impossible, either. Reported *Time* Magazine of the deliberations that ensued: "Tooey was anxious to make a start on his greatest assignment: knocking the props from under the German air force. His plan was ready, with six top-priority factories listed for destruction in the first paralyzing blow. 'It's so important that I would risk the loss of 200 planes,' he said. At 11:30 p.m. Spaatz made his decision. Orders flashed out, and Britain ground crews tumbled out of their bunks throughout their bases to ready the armada—1,600 bombers and fighters. The attack was to mark the beginning of modern precision air war."

The February 19th missions sprung to the sky and the weather was nearly perfect. The bombers that day —and in the days that followed — hit the airframe manufacturing and assembly plants in the cities of Leipzig, Brunswick, Gotha, Regensburg, Schweinfurt, Augsburg and Stuttgart, delivering more than 10,000 tons of bombs.. Good weather followed the next day and the day after that, a week of exceptional conditions for the Allies. Bombers went up again and again. Factories were nearly immobilized by the devastation. More than 1,000 German fighters were shot down or destroyed on the ground. Thousands of tons of bombs rained down on German targets. And while the American losses would total 270 bombers and 103 fighters for the month - more than 2,700 young airmen - Spaatz saw a crack in the wall of Fortress Europe. : "I believe the ability to apply the pressure from two sides against the middle can be utilized to the discomfiture of the enemy," said a confident Spaatz in a cable to Arnold. "My tendency will be to place a little more emphasis upon swatting the enemy on his airdromes whenever possible, then force them to fight under conditions most advantageous to us. There are certain essential targets, however, such as fighter factories and ball-bearing works, which must be hit when weather conditions permit accurate bombing results. These attacks will no doubt result in heavy losses, but they will materially reduce our later losses."

Berlin was next. On March 6 1944, Doolittle launched some 600 heavy bombers and death was visited upon the capital city. Once again the German Air Force mounted fierce opposition, shooting down 69 bombers at the cost of 690 lives but American bombers were over Berlin and the psychological impact was as devastating as the physical destruction. The immediate consequence was a unexpected bonus to the air war commanders—

the Luftwaffe recalled some of their fighters from France, and most of their fighters in Holland and Belgium, to reinforce the defense of Berlin.

By the time of the Berlin raid, more than a third of the German army had been shifted to air defense. The aircraft manufacturing plants, were ringed by hundreds of newly installed antiaircraft batteries with countless barrels pointed skyward, many of them capable of firing 800 rounds a minute. The cities of Berlin and Hamburg, Germany, and Vienna, Austria, had reinforced flak towers built along the air approaches. These hardened towers soared more than 100 feet in height and bristled with guns capable of pouring 8,000 rounds a minute into the sky. Flying around a flak tower was usually impossible due to their effective kill radius of about fourteen miles.

Still, as April 1944 drew to a close, the Eighth Air Force had its battle rhythm. Missions were mounted with a new certainty and it was the rule not the exception to put 500 or more bombers in the air. The sign on Arnold's desk had come to life: "The difficult we do today. The impossible takes a little longer."

The "impossible" was also be the unexpected. On May 9, 1944, an impressive force of 797 American B-17s and B-24s lumbered into the sky and gathered into formations. Flying in battle boxes, they formed a stream more than sixty miles long. On both sides .50 caliber machine guns bristled outwards, tempting the fate of any German who dared to attack. As an added measure, more than 600 fighters flew escort. This time their target was not Berlin. Nor was it Germany.

As the formation crossed the English Channel the navigators proceeded to the east but then unexpectedly and happily, at least to the Germans, turned south. Beginning today, the bombers of the mighty Eighth Air Force would become aerial plow horses and grinders of metal and flesh. They would carve a moot around the D-Day beaches. "This was the start of a new and intense offensive against airfields so that the German Air Force will not have time to recover them before D-Day," wrote author John Ramsey. He may have well written that it was the beginning of victory.

Mission after mission, the bombers of the Eighth cut a no man's land of destruction across France 130 miles wide that stretched from Caen to Normandy. No field would be left uncratered, no aerodrome left standing. Nothing would be sparred that could be used by the Luftwaffe to attack the

D-Day beaches, as the damage report spelled out: "The Paris Orly airfield received 249 tons from 90 B-17's, and a good coverage of the target resulted. Several direct hits were scored on hangars and the west side of the landing area. Bursts blanketed the Lille and Nivelles air fields in France. Some seventy bursts fell in the hangar and barracks area at the west corner. We were virtually unopposed."

The air war generals decisively won the battle of D-Day. Not one bullet was fired by the Luftwaffe against Omaha Beach and scarcely more than a handful of German planes even appeared over Normandy. What by all measure should have been the Luftwaffe's finest hour was instead a day of utter humiliation. The most powerful air force in the world didn't even show up to oppose the landings of D-Day.

The air war generals paid a steep price for air superiority. Between January 1944 and June 1944 over 20,000 airmen were either killed or taken prisoner. But the victory was complete. Several days later, Hap Arnold and General of the Army George Marshall meet Eisenhower for a dinner at Buckingham Palace with Prime Minister Churchill and King George VI. Wrote Arnold in his diary: "It has been three years since I was at Buckingham Palace. I (had) arrived there then just after a heavy GAF bombardment in which considerable damage was done. The king and queen narrowly escaped injury, the windows in the palace were broken, the drafts through the halls made it a most cheerless place. The king was looking for a ray of sunshine. How different now when there is no German threat from land, sea or air. It is a very welcome change, one that everyone has commented on, the results of air supremacy and air power."

In the end Eisenhower said it all as he walked the Normandy beaches with his son, a West Point graduate. Armored trucks and tanks crawled bumper to bumper in a traffic jam as thick as rush hour in Manhattan. Said the young Eisenhower to his father, "You would never get away with this if you didn't have air supremacy."

Said Ike: "If I didn't have air superiority, I wouldn't be here."

About the original manuscript.

War Against the Luftwaffe was written in 1945 by the John F. Ramsey, a young historian on the Army Air Forces staff. Ramsey crafted a tightly chronicled history of the air war and published it just months after the final victory over Germany. The history, however, was not intended for public release and for nearly two decades it remained classified. Once declassified, its existence was unknown to even the most dedicated of WWII historians.

In 2009, a nearly illegible copy was obtained from the Air Force Historical Research Agency and in 2010, a team of technicians and researchers began restoring the document using sophisticated OCR technologies and a little guess work. By and large the words were nursed back to life but there were some exceptions. The original manuscript was written for a military audience and Ramsey often used slang or abbreviations that were well known in 1945 but today are somewhat unclear. To clarify, we provided full names when only a last name was used, we added the names of the countries when only cities were used, and it some cases we added a brief note on what a particular German factory made in order to understand why it was targeted. In a like fashion, we knew that a military audience knew what Operation NOBALL was (the attacks by the Eighth Air Force on the new V-1 rocket sites in France, also known as Crossbow) and that "Salerno Beach" was shorthand for Italy, but we added clarification for today's audience.

Because not all sentences were readable, some editing was necessary. If we couldn't decipher a sentence, we omitted it. In a very few cases we lost entire paragraphs.

In the case of the Bf-109, which was then called the Me-109 but today is called the Bf-109, we used Me-109, as did the author. In the matter of cities, Ramsey was remarkably accurate with the spellings but the passage of time has had its effect. Brazov was then spelled Brasof so for clarity we add the country, Romania, and kept the author's spelling knowing full well that in more than one case a change of one or two letters moved a city from Hungry to Yugoslavia to Bavaria. Then there is the free State of Fiume, where German fighters were based which is now part of Italy and called Rijeka; and Szigetszentmiklos, Hungry, which has several spellings but throughout this book, we retained the author's spelling.

Dr. John Ramsey went on to become a noted historian and the chairman of the department of history at the University of Alabama. In this lost history of World War II, Ramsey pays tribute to the air war victory that was D-

Day. Indeed, the place in history for these brave airmen has now been restored.

1

PLANNING THE AIR OFFENSIVE

As 1940 dawned, the Luftwaffe dominated Europe. After successful battles in Spain (1936-39) and Poland (1939), the German Air Force flew in support of the invasions of Denmark and Norway in April of 1940, then crushed the French aerial resistance in the brief weeks of the Battle of France in May. As the summer of 1940 drew near, the Luftwaffe poised triumphantly on the edge of the Channel ready to launch what would become known as the Battle of Britain.

During these incredible months of seemingly unstoppable control of the air, when the prestige of German arms had reached the highest point, the German Air Force (GAF) was a formidable weapon. The Stuka dive bomber provided the infantry with a new weapon far more effective for certain purposes than even artillery. The basic German fighter, the light and fast Messerschmitt 109, called the Me-109, seemed superior to any plane that could be brought against it until the Battle of Britain revealed its weaknesses in armor, fire power and aerial maneuverability.

Thus in 1940, the GAF, the dominant air power in Europe, struck England only to receive its first defeat, this at the hands of the RAF - the Royal Air Force. Anti-aircraft fire-control devices such as radar proved fatal to the close formations of German bombers, while the Chain Home radar stations provided the RAF with early warnings necessary for launching its Spitfires.

The German bomber and fighters were unable to stand up against the heavy armament of the British Spitfires or the nimble maneuvers employed by its pilots.

Following the defeat of the GAF over Britain, a change was noticeable in the composition of the Luftwaffe. An immediate emphasis on fighters was carried out to the virtual extinction of the bomber command. Why this change occurred is not yet clear. One source attributes it to the losses of German planes in the Battle of Britain, plus the need for creating a defensive force of fighters to protect the German industry against the night raids of the RAF. On the other hand, German Field Marshall Hermann Goering, commander of the Luftwaffe, stated that it was not the losses over London that caused the increase in German fighter production, but rather the preparations for the campaign against the U.S.S.R. Owing to the lack of industrial concentrations suitable for the employment of bombers, Goering said that the demand for bombers thus decreased, while the demand for fighters considerably increased.

Whatever the underlying causes, the summer of 1940 saw two important developments in the German fighter command: (1) the appearance of a "souped-up" version of the Me-109 and (2) the design of a new and improved fighter. The new versions of the Me-109 were faster, armored, and provided with better firepower. For example, the Me-109F had a cannon firing through the propeller hub in addition to the machine guns. The G model, which became operational late in 1942, kept the cannon and increased the fire power of the two machine guns to approximately .50 caliber with 900 rounds each. The plane had an enormous 1,700 horsepower engine and was believed to have a service ceiling of nearly 40,000 feet. It had a speed of more than 400 miles per hour.

The new fighter was the Focke-Wulf 190 (FW-190). The original version had a maximum speed of 385 m.p.h. at 17,000 feet, and could climb to 18,000 feet in six minutes. It had a ceiling of 36,000 feet, was protected with 197 pounds of armor, and was armed with two low-velocity 20-mm. cannons and two machine guns. Later models were designed for ground attack and carried extra guns, with as much as 792 pounds of armor plate around the pilot and on the bottom of the fuselage. It was possible the Germans had devised a fighter superior to any plane that might oppose it. Little wonder that the first appearance of the Focke-Wulf 190 late in 1941 created something of a sensation - as well as a sense of urgency - among Allied war planners.

However, after coming off the drawing boards as it did in mid-1940, it presented a serious production problem for the Germans. Producing the plane for wartime consumption required manufacturing capacity of which there were three alternatives. The fighter could be built in new plants constructed for that purpose, but this would involve at least a year's delay as well as result in heavy costs and manpower shortages. A second alternative was to convert other general fighter factories to the production of the new fighter. This plan had the advantage of being somewhat easier to set up, but it had the decided disadvantage of slowing down the output of other types of aircraft. The third alternative, which was eventually adopted, was to simply convert certain Me-109 plants to the manufacture of the FW-190. Since many of the same tools would do for the new plane, and the workmen would be accustomed to building a similar type, this idea was considered the simplest and most practicable of the three.

At the beginning of 1941, the Me-109 was produced in five German plants and one Austrian: (1) the Fieseler airplane plant in Kassel, Germany; (2) the Arado airplane factories in Warnemunde, Germany; (3) AGO plants, in Oschersleben, Germany; (4) the Messerschmitt complex in Regensburg, Germany; (5) the Erla plants in Leipzig, Germany; and (6) the Messerschmitt complex in Wiener Neustadt, Austria. The first four were producing forty to fifty fighters per month, and the last two produced between sixty to seventy-five. It was finally decided to convert the first three to the production of FW-190s because it would involve a smaller loss of output, for the plants concerned were closer than the others to the parent Focke-Wulf plant at Bremen. This arrangement was believed to be the most efficient for the subcontractors. Accordingly, estimate showed that by November, Me-109 production had dropped to 260 per month while the output of the FW-190 fighter had risen to 220 monthly, thus bringing the total construction of single-engine fighters to 480 per month.

#

It appears that the final decision to build up a huge fighter force was reached in the middle of 1942. Hitler's Soviet adventure was not proceeding according to schedule, and the scope of the campaign was constantly increasing. The largest part of the German fighter command was flying on the Eastern front, and more and more planes were constantly needed. Meanwhile, a new menace had arisen in the West. The RAF, supposedly driven out of the skies during 1940 and 1941, was beginning to be a threat with its night bombing. Finally, the B-17 Flying Fortresses of the U. S. Eighth Air Force made its first appearance over German-held territory at Rouen, France, on 17 August 1942. All of this made it clear that in addition to the requirements of the war in the East, it would be necessary to develop a large fighter strength in the west to protect German cities and its war industries. Since the bulk of German air power was then concentrated on the Eastern front, the increased production of fighter aircraft would solve both problems—this was the solution.

In the middle of 1942, elaborate plans were being made for a tremendous increase in the production of German fighter aircraft. A committee had been formed under Field Marshall Goering to speed up industry; by December of 1944, many hoped planes would be coming off the assembly lines at a rate of 2,000 per month. This could be brought about by a reorganization of aircraft production. Previously, the industry consisted of a large number of firms each making their own components, then assembling a small number of aircraft; further expansion along these lines seemed blocked by both the labor shortage and also the fact that the supply of skilled craftsmen had been considerably diluted by the importation of unskilled foreign workers. Goering's committee decided to reorganize the industry by breaking down working procedures to the simplest stages. Some factories switched to the making of components; others were to specialize in the assembly of the finished products. Geographically, production was to be centered in a few great complexes consisting of an assembly plant surrounded by various component factories within a 50-mile radius feeding their products into the central assembly. That such a scheme was vulnerable to air attack was well realized. At the time the production setup was reorganized, however, the Germans believed that the Allies could not conduct long range missions without unacceptable losses and that strategic precision bombing would be ineffective.

#

With the introduction of a new fighter and the reorganization of production, the first phase in the expansion of the German fighter command was well under way in mid-1942. A second phase was inaugurated in the fall of 1942 when an increase in the construction of the Me-109 began. Earlier rumors that the FW-190 was going to replace the older fighter plane were killed by the unusually successful performance of the G model, which the Messerschmitt complex at Wiener Neustadt was producing as early as the summer of 1942. Estimated production at this time was eighty to ninety planes a month; but at the close of summer, all the plants making the Me-109 unexpectedly began a tremendous increase of production. The Wiener Neustadt facilities progressively increased their output until they were building 220 fighters a month (June 1943), representing an increase of 150% over 1942 production. Since this complex was 800 air miles from London, the Germans felt the chances of being bombed were relatively remote.

At Regensburg, the output of Me-109's was at forty-five per month; however, by November 1942, it was increased to seventy-five. By June of 1943, it was believed to have reached two hundred. By this time, these huge complexes at Regensburg and Wiener Neustadt were producing fifty-five percent of all single-engine planes used by the GAF. During this same period, the third Messerschmitt plant, the Erla plant at Leipzig, showed an increase in product of fifty percent.

While the output of the Me-109 climbed rapidly, that of the FW-190 showed surprisingly little fluctuation between November 1942 and June 1943. According to an OSS report, this stabilization may have been caused by the physical relocation of certain factories to the safer eastern part of the Reich. It is possible the heavy RAF raids in 1942 hastened this by convincing the German leaders that western factories would be too exposed, for the three production centers of Kassel, Oschersleben, and Bremen averaged only 402 great circle miles from London, with Warnemunde somewhat farther to the east. The apparent failure of the Germans to repair the damage caused by the Eighth Air Force raid on Bremen 17 April 1943 suggests the assembly of FW-190's had been transferred to eastern Germany.

Meanwhile, the production of aero-engines developed along the same lines as airframe factories. Wherever possible, a central assembly factory was surrounded with its own satellite component plants. However, between 1943 and 1944, a serious shortage of raw materials hampered the aero-engine industry, especially those used in hardening steel. Additionally, RAF night raids on Cologne, Essen, and Hamburg knocked out certain plants producing crankshaft forgings; as a result, there was a backlog of engines awaiting these parts.

#

To summarize, regardless of what minor inroads the Allies made to reduce production of fighters, by the middle of 1943 German fighter production and the massing of German planes in the West were causing serious concern among the British and American planners. In June, it was estimated that 550 Me-109's and 230 FW-190's would be produced alone, not to mention a wide array of other models, all of which could be employed effectively against our bomber sorties. Furthermore, there had been a steady shift of GAF units from the East to the West, and another fighter wing, the 11th Jagdgeschwader, had been formed to check strategic bombers operating from England. According to American estimates, the GAF order of battle early in 1943 showed the following distribution:

Axis Air Strength	Total Combat and Miscellaneous Aircraft
Western front	1320
Mediterranean (and Italy)	1248
Central Germany	732
Russian front	2460

Not only was the force in the West a major threat to strategic bombardment, but, if not destroyed, it could also be greatly augmented by reinforcements from other areas when the threat of an invasion became imminent.

Thus, at the close of 1942, one source estimated the amount of air power, which the GAF could mass against a cross-Channel operation such as D-Day, was approximately 3,700 planes. All of these factors made it clear that concerted action must be taken by both British and American air forces to drive the Luftwaffe out of the skies in order to pave the way for an invasion of Hitler's Festung Europa.

The RAF, though, had already a good start. In addition to strategic bombing, two types of operations, known by the code names RHUBARB and CIRCUS, were underway. These operations were mounted with the express purpose of inducing the enemy to commit his fighters to battle in the hopes of destroying them in combat. In RHUBARB operations, heavily armed fighters and fighter-bombers operated within a 150-mile radius of the RAF forward fighter stations against enemy installations near the Channel coast. By striking at ground targets of considerable value to the enemy, such as transportation and port installations, many hoped the Luftwaffe would be forced to give battle to protect them.

Though similar, CIRCUS operations involved the medium bombers of No. 2 Group RAF; later, it was hoped to use the Marauders of the 3d Bombardment Wing (Eighth Air Force) when this organization became operational. Targets were selected within an area of 150 to 180 miles from forward bases. According to British authorities, the "prime object of the operations is again to destroy [the enemy] fighter by our fighter aircraft rather than to inflict any serious economic damage on his war machine in the industrial sense...." American fighters - and later medium bombers - were ordered to take part in RHUBARB and CIRCUS missions as a means of acquainting new units with combat conditions in the theater. It was doubtful that these missions seriously threatened the German Air Force or menaced the Third Reich. As time went on, the enemy often refused to commit its fighters to coastal missions.

#

As the Eighth Air Force became operational in England, attacks by its heavy bombers in the latter half of 1942 were more effective in terms of damaging the German war machinery; still, these raids were more useful as indications of future activity than as true gains in the war against Germany. Not only had bad weather interfered with many of the missions during the second half of 1942, but the Eighth had also been forced to divert much of its equipment and crews to the newly formed Twelfth Air Force in North African. Partly because of this, the planned build-up of planes in the United Kingdom lagged behind schedule. Moreover, replacement aircraft and crews were lacking, and the personnel that did arrive from the United States generally required considerable training, plus bombers required weeks of final modifications before they could be used in operations. As a result, the build-up of American air power was painfully slow. As late as April of 1943, American units in England had only 264 heavy bombers (198 B-17s and 66 B-24s) and 172 P-47s.

#

Despite the slow build-up, April 1943 marked the first major advance in the war against the Luftwaffe with the formation of the Combined Bomber Offensive Plan (CBO Plan). This document, which provided for the build-up and operation of a large bomber force based in England, was the culmination of much thought on the proper use of air power. While German air doctrine tended to emphasize tactical operations in close support of the ground forces, both the RAF and the AAF were anxious to exploit the possibilities of strategic bombardment. For the first time in the history of war, bombing would be conducted entirely independent of ground or naval operations.

In the United States General Billy Mitchell's doctrines of strategic aerial bombing had been accepted by the Air Corps and received further development at the hands of the very pioneers in air strategy, including Commanding General of the Army Air Force General Henry "Hap" Arnold, strategic bombing advocate, Casablanca committee member General Frank Maxwell Andrews, now commander of United States Forces in Europe, General Ira G. Eaker, newly installed commander of the Eighth Air Force, and General Carl A. "Tooey" Spaatz, Commander of the Army Air Force Operations in Europe. On 9 July 1941, when President Roosevelt asked the secretary of war to prepare a plan for overall production requirements needed to defeat our possible enemies, these air strategists put forward their concepts of modern aerial warfare: the Air War Plans Division plan 1.

The air document, generally known by its short title of AWPD/1, was submitted on 12 August and was broadly conceived. The section covering air production called for 60,000 planes and envisaged an air war of three phases culminating with a great intensification of air operations to ensure air supremacy prior to an invasion of German-held territory. Targets for bombardment included electrical installations such as power lines and hydro-electric stations, transportation systems, oil producing centers, and industrial plants. It was also recognized that before these objectives could be attacked, it might be necessary first to neutralize the Luftwaffe by "employing large numbers of aircraft with high speed, good defensive fire power, and high altitude." It would also be necessary to make deep penetrations into the Reich to attack airfields, aluminum plants and aircraft factories. This document is important for recognizing that an indispensable preliminary to an invasion of the Continent was eliminating German air power. It is also significant for clearly establishing the attack on the GAF was a double operation, an attack not only against the sources of aircraft production but also against units of the Luftwaffe at their bases. It also recommended that plans be undertaken towards the formation of heavily armed escort fighters that would fly alongside and protect the bombers.

After being accepted as a basis for further planning in September, the document was followed by a broad discussion of overall strategy between the top British and American authorities. After the Japanese attack on Pearl Harbor, many details were naturally altered due to the exigencies of the crisis in which the United States found itself; however, the basic ideas embodied in AWPD/1 remained largely unchanged and were repeated in a later modification of the project known as AWPD/42. General Arnold drew up this plan in response to a request on 24 August 1942 from the president to his military authorities for a statement of the needs of the Army, Navy, and, lend-lease, "in order to have complete air ascendency over the enemy." In his reply for the AAF, General Arnold listed a series of air operations beginning with "an air offensive against Europe to deplete the GAF, destroy the sources of German submarine construction, and undermine the German war-making capacity." Ascendency was defined as the depletion of the enemy air force to such an extent as to render it incapable of resisting the offensive of land, sea and air forces.

A first priority in the air offensive was to attack the Luftwaffe. To eliminate it from combat, AWPD/42 called for a total of 22,374 sorties that would drop 44,748 tons against 11 fighter factories, 15 bomber factories and 17 aero-engine plants. To attain complete destruction of these plants, attacks were to be repeated where necessary at two-month intervals. Combat attrition, that is, engaging the enemy and destroying it on the front-line, was to complete the destruction of the GAF. The timetable in the plan called for six months of all-out operations at full strength. One-third of the job was to be completed in 1943, thereby requiring four additional months of 1944. If all went well, General Arnold believed that the Luftwaffe could be eliminated as a threat to our forces by May of 1944, with cross-channel operations beginning soon after. Later developments were to prove the remarkable accuracy of AWFD/42's timetable.

#

The final phase of planning for the attack on the GAF began on 9 December 1942 when a Committee of Operations Analysts (COA) was set up by General Arnold. The Analysts were asked to define target systems that were weak links in the German war industry and would provide the most disruption if destroyed. This committee, comprised of civilian and military analysts, were also required to prepare a report analyzing the rate of "progressive deterioration" that should be anticipated as a result of the operations against Germany's "sustaining sources," as Arnold's directive stated. On 8 March 1943, after some months of intensive study, the committee submitted their report, which was remarkably similar to the final form of the CBO Plan. This report did not depart from the general principles of an air offensive against the Reich as laid down in AWFD/1 and AWFD/42, but it succeeded in giving these doctrines their most elaborate application based on what was then available in planes, crews, and time, as well as indicating what build-up of forces would be necessary to carry the offensive to a successful conclusion. The committee recognized the desirability of carrying out precision attacks against the German fighter assembly plants and engine factories, but felt the present build-up of heavy bombers with units in the theater (264 as of April) was insufficient to make the necessary deep penetration flights. The committee felt a minimum force of 300 bombers would be needed to organize the requisite diversions and penetrate the heavily defended targets. (Of the 300 bombers, 50 were to form a diversionary force to hold down a part of the German fighter strength, 200 were to constitute the main striking force, and the remaining 50 were to divert the German fighters while the bombers were withdrawing from the target area.) An estimated 800 bombers in the theater were needed to keep 300 constantly in operation. Until this build-up could be achieved, the COA did not recommend mounting a large-scale offensive against aircraft factories, but instead advised that missions concentrate on repair depots, U-boat bases, and the few factories located by the coast.

It was hoped that by July, the bomber strength would be augmented to the point where deep penetrations of 400 miles could be realized; in this second phase of the offensive, the committee recommended a heavy concentration of attacks on GAF fighter factories. Here was where the experts disagreed. In considering the German aircraft industry, the COA had examined the possibility of attacking (1) airframe components, (2) engine components, (3) fighter assembly plants, and (4) engine assembly plants. The principal disagreement was whether the heaviest attack should be directed against fighter assembly plants or fighter-engine assembly plants. Those favoring an attack on fighter assemblies pointed out that the GAF had to recreate itself approximately every three months, and that the destruction of seven assembly plants, even if remediable within thirty days, would have only to be repeated twice to effect a substantial reduction of GAF strength.

The opponents of this view were disturbed by the high recuperative ability of the fighter assembly plants. They were concerned that not enough damage could be done to put them out of production for any long period of time. On the other hand, they held that engine assembly plants could be put out of action for at least six months. Furthermore, five plants accounted for all the BMW engines used in the FW-190, and another five plants produced the DB motor used in the Me-109, -110, and -210. Consequently, a comparatively small number of targets might, if thoroughly bombed, upset a large part of the German fighter production. The COA did not attempt to solve the dispute and in later operations, the combined bomber forces attacked both fighter assembly and engine assembly plants. (The comment of a captured German field marshal on this point is interesting: "As the brunt of the attacks throughout July, August, September, and October 1943 was borne by the aircraft industry, naturally that suffered most. Fortunately you didn't do one thing: you didn't attack our engine production on a large scale - a much more vulnerable branch. Instead you went for the airframe plants.")

#

The final form of the CBO Plan, which was completed in the first of April, consisted of a carefully selected list of target systems coordinated with the expected build-up of bomber strength in the theater, along with a timetable. The main purpose of the plan was to carry out the directive of the Combined Chiefs of Staff at the Casablanca meeting: to "accomplish the progressive destruction and dislocation of the German military, industrial and economic system, and the undermining of the morale of the German people to a point where their capacity for armed resistance is fatally weakened." The targets designated for attack were submarine construction yards and bases, German aircraft industry, ball bearings, oil, synthetic rubber, and military transport vehicles. The determination of the number of bombers needed to accomplish the CBO Plan was based on a yardstick derived from previous operations of the Eighth Air Force. Twelve successful missions were mounted in January, February, and March, using approximately 100 bombers on each target. Important data were generated, including circular errors and acceptable bombing patterns. Said one analyst:

```
"It was found that sufficient bombs fell within a circle of 1,000 foot
radius centered about the aiming point to cause the desired destruction.
Thus, for each prospective target, the number of 1,000 foot radius circles
necessary to cover it has been calculated. The yardstick as determined by
experience is therefore: the number of 1,000 foot radius circles of
destruction to destroy a given target times 100 bombers for each radius."
```

To carry out successful missions against the six target systems, using the ratio indicated above, the CBO required the following build-up of U.S. heavy and medium bombers in the United Kingdom:

30 June 1943	944 Heavy 200 Medium
30 Sep 1943	1192 Heavy 400 Medium
31 Dec 1943	1746 Heavy 600 Medium
31 Mar 1944	2702 Heavy 800 Medium

The operational timetable of the offensive was divided into four phases. The first phase ended on 1 July 1943 and was based on the assumptions that no more than 300 bombers would be continually in operations and the operational range would be 300 miles. The main emphasis was to be placed on striking U-boat bases.

The second phase from July to October was to be principally against the fighter aircraft industries. The radius of action was to be extended to 400 miles, and the 1,192 bombers in the theater were expected to provide an average striking force of 450 planes. While the Fortresses and Liberators were hitting the main objectives, the mediums were to mount diversionary attacks on German-held airfields within their limited range.

In the third phase, from October to January 1944, the German fighter force was to be kept depleted; in aaddition to the aircraft industry, oil, transportation and rubber facilities were to be attacked. The average striking force during this phase was to be about 550 bombers.

In the fourth phase in early 1944, the principal objective would be to sustain the previous affects achieved and pave the way for the invasion of the Continent.

The committee recognized the immediate danger to their plans from the German fighter force in the West; its destruction was to be "an intermediate objective second to none in priority." Furthermore, the Plan emphasized in italics the statement that:

"If the growth of the German fighter strength is not arrested quickly, it may become literally impossible to carry out the destruction planned and thus to create the conditions necessary for ultimate decisive action by our combined forces on the Continent. Hence, the successful prosecution of the air offensive against the principal objectives is dependent upon a prior (or simultaneous) offensive against German fighter strength."

Though completed by the COA in Washington, the Plan appears to have been coordinated with British and American authorities in the theater. This is evident by RAF Air Marshal Sir Charles Portal's writing to General Arnold of his full approval on 15 April 1943. Here he stated the Commander in Chief of the RAF Bomber Command has seen the plan and was also "convinced of its soundness and importance." Portal urged that "every effort ... be made to achieve and if possible to exceed the program." Final approval came from the Combined Chiefs of Staff on 19 May 1943.

The CBO Plan, although recognizing the immediate importance of checking the growth of the German Air Force in the West, nevertheless dealt with it as only one of several important objectives. As indicated by a British plan developed concurrently with the CBO Plan, British thought at the time was more concerned with checking the growth of German fighters by striking at airdromes, repair installations, and Messerschmitt and Focke-Wulf factories. Entitled "The Attack on the GAF," this document stated:

```
"The most formidable weapon being used by the enemy today against our
bomber offensive is his Fighter Force—his single-engine fighters by day
and his twin-engine fighters by night—and the elimination or serious
depletion of this force would be the greatest contribution to the
furtherance of the joint heavy bomber offensive of the RAF and the AAF."
```

This document then called for an attack on the sources of fighter strength—airfields and factories. It is evident that the authors of the plan assumed medium bombers and fighters would conduct most of the attacks on the fields, although several such missions had already been mounted by the heavy bombers of the Eighth Air Force. Since some 34 GAF airfields housing about 465 aircraft were within range of RHUBARB and CIRCUS operations, the study recommended they be promptly attacked. The fields at Rennes, (St. Jacques Airport), Caen, (Carpiquet Airport), Lille (Vende-ville), and Vitry-en-Artois, France; the field at Courtrai, Belgium (Nevel-ghem Field); the field in Beaumont-le-Roger, Bernay, Evreux, Cherbourg, Merville, and Brest, France the airports in Amsterdam, Netherlands (Schi-phol Airport), and Woensdrecht, Netherlands, were pointed out as being especially important. AAF units later attacked most of these fields.

After careful study of the capabilities and limitations of the heavy bomber, ten towns were listed in the plan as "tactically suitable" for attack by high-level precision daylight bombing by the Eight Air Force's VIII Bomber Command, then followed by RAF night attacks. These towns were Bremen (FW-190 assembly), Brunswick (Me-110 assembly and DB-605 engine plant), Kassel (FW-190 assembly), Hamburg (BMW engines), Schweinfurt (ball-bearing works), Hanover (aero-tire works), Stuttgart (important aircraft components), Gotha (Me-110 assembly), Eisenach (aero-engines), and Oschersleben (FW-190 assembly). As in the case of the airfields noted above, these aircraft factories were later attacked heavily by the AAF VIII Bomber Command.

#

By the beginning of April 1943, the stage was set for a great air battle. The Germans had committed themselves to a program of fighter construction that definitely threatened the success of the combined strategic bomber offensive and the attack on the Continent. To check this development, the British and American air strategists were planning nothing less than the destruction of the Luftwaffe and its exclusion from the air over Europe. This was to be accomplished by a double attack: on one hand, German aircraft factories were to be destroyed once the build-up of strength permitted deep penetrations; on the other hand, the Luftwaffe was to be forced to commit itself to battle wherever it could be found, either on the ground or by air. It was now the task of the AAF and the RAF to prove that Hitler's Festung Europa was, indeed, a fortress without a roof.

2

THE FIRST OPERATIONS AGAINST THE LUFTWAFFE

Although the combined Chiefs of Staff did not formally approve the CBO plan until the middle of May 1943, attacks on German aircraft production commenced in April. During the first quarter of the new year, the Chiefs dispatched 1,681 sorties with claims of 263 enemy aircraft shot down. As anticipated, the bomber strength was too meager to sustain deep penetrations into the heart of Germany where the bulk of the aircraft industry was located. However, installations near England could be attacked with small concentrations in comparative safety.

Such a mission was carried out on 5 April 1943. The target was the Erla Aircraft and Aero-Engine Repair works near Antwerp, Belgium, only about 190 miles from the nearest English bases. Out of 104 planes airborne, 64 B-17's and 18 B-24's dropped 240.5 tons of 1,000- and 500-1b. General Purpose (GP) bombs with fair results. Damage was done to an assembly shop, and some repair installations were set on fire. Four bombers were lost and claims of twenty-three enemy aircraft destroyed, eight probable, and four damaged were made (usually indicated in this history as "23-8-4"). In this rather unimpressive manner, the bomber offensive against German aircraft production began, a series of missions called POINTBLANK. POINT-BLANK was the official codename for attacks on German aircraft production centers and supporting plants that made, for example, ball bearings, along with German fighters and fighter bases on the frontlines.

The next POINTBLANK mission was carried out on 17 April when 115 bombers were dispatched to strike at the Focke-Wulf fighter assembly plant at a distance of two and one-half miles from the center of Bremen. This mission was considered especially important since the FW factory here was the parent producer of the FW-190 single-engine fighter. Its estimated production of 80 planes per month was believed to be 35 percent of all FW-190's produced. (The FW assembly at Bremen was ultimately moved to Marienburg, but it is not yet clear whether or not this move had taken place at the time of the 17 April raid. Later the British believed that it had already taken place. However, when Goering was interrogated after being taken prisoner, he stated the April raid had inflicted damage on FW assembly at Bremen, thereby indicating it was still there.) In addition to the FW plant, there was also a Junkers assembly plant, and a components factory nearby.

The mission was run off under somewhat adverse conditions. The weather was hazy, making target identification difficult; the excellent camouflage used by the Germans added to the problems of the bombardiers. Furthermore, the flak was of a concentration heretofore unknown. According to the Tactical Mission Report:

"The intensity of the flak was probably the most severe that has ever been experienced by this Wing, and the huge volume of smoke that overhung the target area while our later Groups were approaching acted as a very real deterrent, causing many members of combat crews to feel it would be an impossibility to fly in the area without suffering damage. Although only one plane appears to have been actually destroyed by flak, forty-three others sustained battle damage."

It had been expected that the Luftwaffe would rush to the defense of such an important target—and such proved to be the case. Combat crews estimated that some 150 enemy aircraft took the air against the bombers, and attacks began, while the formations were passing over the Frisian Islands and becoming more and more intense as the target was approached. To meet these attacks, the three elements of each combat wing were flown in a vertical wedge with a permanent group leading. Another permanent group was slightly below and behind to obtain support from the nose guns and ball turrets of the lead group. The 102d Wing managed to maintain a close formation of this type and was able to present such a wall of fire to approaching enemy fighters that most were discouraged and failed to press home their strikes. Unfortunately, the 101st Wing failed to fly a tight formation and received the brunt of the attacks, resulting in a heavy loss of 16 bombers. All types of enemy aircraft were seen, but most of the attacks came from FW-190's and Me-109's. Twin-engine fighters did not attack directly but instead paced the formations at a distance waiting to pounce on stragglers.

In spite of this violent opposition, 107 Fortresses out of the 115 dispatched managed to bomb the target with 531 x 1,000-1b. GP; although all the bombs fell to the right of the aiming point, the results were considered satisfactory. Considerable damage to the central and east part of the assembly works was reported. Buildings hit included a hangar, the component erecting shop, an assembly shop or flight hangar, the firing range, a paint shop or inspection hangar, a boiler house, and a coal dump. Numerous fires were started. Approximately one-half of the factory was destroyed. It was estimated that about fifty enemy aircraft were shot down, with approximately fifteen probables and seventeen damaged. Four squadrons of Spitfires furnished withdrawal support, and a Typhoon squadron made a diversionary sweep. (Claims of enemy fighters shot down can only be regarded as approximations. Not only are the figures suspected of being much too high, but there is also considerable disagreement among various theater sources. Thus, in the mission referred to, the VIII Bomber Command claims sixty-three destroyed, fifteen likely destroyed, and seventeen damaged, while the Tactical Mission Report for this operation cites 47-17-10 as claims.)

Taking into account battle damage, a total of fifty-nine bombers were hit or destroyed. Thus, following the Bremen mission, attacks against GAF targets were suspended for almost a month. In the meantime there was a considerable increase in B-17s (from 198 to 331 with units), and the P-47 fighter became operational and went on its first bomber-escort mission on 5 May 1943. However, the VIII Fighter Command remained relatively weak for some months to come; by July, there were only 195 American fighter planes in the theater, with the bulk of the escort work borne by the RAF.

May was a far better month operationally than April. A total of 2,677 tons of bombs were dropped, as compared with the 1,130 in the previous month. Most of the targets were submarine bases, building yards and Luftwaffe installations. Some eleven of the objectives were specified in the CBO Plan. A total of 380 enemy aircraft were listed as destroyed of which VIII Bomber Command claims were 372-93-176.

The only direct blow during the month against GAF bases occurred on the 13th. On this date, a force of 169 B-17's were dispatched against the Potez Aircraft Repair Depot at Meaulte, France, and the Fort Rouge and Longuenesse airdromes at St. Omer in Pas de Calais, France. The Potez aircraft plant was currently engaged in fuselage manufacture and repair works for the Dornier 245 (Do-245); it was evidently considered an important target, for it had been raided three times previously. It was also fewer than 200 miles distant from British bases. The mission was only partly successful, in spite of there being excellent fighter support and practically no opposition. The bombing at St. Omer was poor, but at Meaulte there were good concentrations on and around the target; it was believed that considerable damage had been done to installations. Four bombers were lost and eleven enemy fighters were claimed destroyed.

Once again a long pause followed. Most of the emphasis was now being placed on submarine installations, and it was not until 26 June that the Eighth Air Force turned again to strike directly at GAF airdromes. The results were less than successful. The two hundred and forty-six Fortresses sent out against targets in France would run into bad weather; as a result, 161 returned without dropping a bomb. A small force of twelve managed to drop 112 x 500-lb. GP bombs on the airdrome at Villacoublay, France, which was a repair, maintenance, and assembly center for the German Junkers and French Caudron aircraft. A few planes bombed the Poissy airfield in France. As a secondary effort, thirty-nine heavy bombers attempted to bomb the field at Tocqueville, France. On all these missions, the results were negative. Two days later, a force of forty-three planes dropped 688 x 300 lb. GP bombs on the field at Beaumont-le-Roger with a good concentration on the west dispersal area. The next day, 74 B-17s made what was then considered a deep penetration to hit the Gnome et Rhone Aero

Engine Works at Le Mans, France, with poor results. This operation closed the rather disappointing month.

#

Although the rising strength of 582 bombers represented the largest number of American Liberators and Flying Fortresses yet assembled in the United Kingdom, the June operations fell below the level of May. The bomb load was some two hundred tons lower, and the claims were less. Losses were relatively high at eight percent of the total bombers over the target, while the capacity of the Luftwaffe to produce seemed unaffected. The estimated production of the Me-109 and the FW-190 reached a total of 770 for the month, and there was evidence that July's output would be even higher. As long as this production level could be maintained, the loss of 788 planes, which the Eighth claimed to have shot down in the second quarter of 1943, would not be seriously felt. No doubt this situation caused the authorities in Washington serious concern for early in June, General Arnold was pressing General Baker to get more bombers into combat. However, it was not until July and August that the POINTBLANK operations assumed the leading role in the CBO.

July showed improvements and was an important month in the war against the Luftwaffe, although the transfer of three B-24 groups to another theater handicapped the operations. In addition, weather seriously interfered with the selection of high-priority targets, forcing the bombers to concentrate on objectives nearer at hand. Nevertheless, in spite of this weather difficulty, the time was well employed, for the Eighth unleashed a series of vigorous attacks against Luftwaffe bases and repair centers. The official report for July characterized these raids on the German fighter force on the ground as "the first serious offensive of this kind to which he had been exposed." On 4 July the first of these missions against GAF ground installations took place when 103 bombers visited Le Mans, with 61 attacking the Heinkel III repair and component plant at Nantes, France. Four planes were lost over Le Mans and three at Nantes; the total claims for both operations were 53-13-22 enemy fighters. Weather prevented further missions until 10 July when the Eighth struck again at airfields. Plans to attack the important repair center at Villacoublay were forestalled by a heavy overcast, but the 1st Wing bombed Caen and Abbeville airdromes with thirty-one and thirty-eight planes respectively. The results were classified as good.

Uncertain weather conditions again prevailed over the interior of the Continent during the second week of July; consequently, the mission planned for the 14th was against more airfields. Early in the morning, 101 bombers of the 1st Wing made the now familiar run to Villacoublay, blasting the target with a heavy load of 500 and 1,000-1b. GP bombs. The results were excellent. The aiming point was completely covered with bursts, and the target was demolished. A large number of planes were destroyed in the hangars. Smaller forces raided the Amiens-Glissy airfield and Le Bourget airfield in France with good results, although persistent attacks by enemy fighters caused some overrunning of the target at Le Bourget. Although fully justified by results, this raid was more costly than the previous ones, and it was evident that German opposition was increasing. Eight bombers failed to return, and the air battles were numerous and fierce as the high bomber claims of 65-35-51 indicated.

A new type of operation was carried out on the 16th when 36 B-26 bombers of the newly organized VIII Air Support Command assisted by 129 P-47's were dispatched in a sweep over occupied territory. This marked the beginning of a long series of attacks on GAF airdromes as diversions to the deeper penetrations of the heavy bombers.

#

With a slight improvement of weather conditions, the VIII Bomber Command planned deeper penetrations of German territory for the 17th and 25th, but conditions were not completely favorable until the 28th. Beginning with that date, three important missions were sent deep into Germany. Mission No. 78 on 28 July was directed against FW-190 production at Kassel and Oschersleben. Kassel was a high-priority target area with two important objectives for heavy-bomber attack. Of prime importance was the Fieseler Aircraft Assembly works at Waldau, Germany, about three miles southeast of the center of Kassel. This factory was an important producer of the FW-190 and, at the time of the raid, it was believed to be producing fifty aircraft per month, or twenty-two percent of the total production of this type. Five miles southwest of the city in the suburb of Alenbauna, Germany, lay the Henschel Aero Engine Works, an important producer of the DB-601 and -605 engines used in the Me-109, and Me-110 and -210 twin-engine fighters. The output of the Henschel factory was believed to account for twenty-five percent of the total production of these important engines. The main target at Oschersleben was the Ago Aircraft Assembly Works situated on the outskirts of the town. Its production was approximately equal to Fieseler's output. With good luck, the VIII Bomber Command might hope for the partial elimination of forty-four percent of FW-190 production.

Unfortunately, luck did not attend the 78th mission. Although carefully planned, things went wrong from the start. The 4th Wing, which was involved in an elaborate feint toward the Hamburg area to cause the enemy controllers to divide his fighters, had navigational difficulties and came too close to the Danish peninsula, "result[ing] in an attack by enemy fighters during the feint instead of forcing (them) to land and refuel as they ha[d] done in the past." The weather deteriorated as the mission proceeded and of the impressive force of 302 bombers dispatched, only 77 were able to bomb the targets assigned, while only 17 were able to strike opportunity targets in northwest Germany. The results at Kassel were fair. There was a heavy concentration of hits on workers' living quarters at the Fieseler plant, and another burst in the corner of the Spinnfaser Textile Mill. Flak was intense, and of the seven bombers lost over this target, three were completely destroyed.

Twenty-eight B-17's of the 2d Wing attacked Oschersleben, as they dropped 500-lb.GP and incendiary bombs. Although smoke and clouds obscured the aiming point, many hits landed in the target area, with several buildings destroyed. Flak was much lighter here, but enemy fighter opposition was correspondingly more intense and fifteen of the Forts were destroyed. The total loss of twenty-two bombers made this one of the most costly raids to date. Three bombers were hit and destroyed by air-to-air bombing—a device often tried by the Germans but usually ineffective. This raid was one of the few occasions where it appears to have worked. Total claims of 86-33-66, even though unduly high, indicate the Forts gave a good account of themselves; the fact that two more heavy missions were immediately prepared indicates morale had not suffered.

The following day, a force of ninety-five bombers bombed Kiel, Germany, while forty-four attacked targets of opportunity; fifty-four hit Warnemunde as a diversion for the other forces. The target at Warnemunde was the Ernest Heinkel Airframe Factory, which received a severe bombing. Direct hits were scored on most of the main buildings, including workshops, storage buildings, assembly plants, offices, and boiler shops. A final estimate of damage made on 4 August showed that eighteen out of the twenty-seven buildings had been hit, and twelve could be counted as destroyed or severely damaged. This achievement of the 4th Wing at Warnemunde showed what could be accomplished under favorable conditions with daylight precision bombing.

The last mission of the month was run off on the 30th. A force of 186 aircraft from the 1st and 4th Wings took off for a second mission against the Fieseler plant at Kassel. This raid proved to be more successful than the previous mission of 28 July; 131 bombers reached the objective, and the bombing was good. The 1st Wing seriously damaged two buildings, setting off a violent explosion that caused a column of smoke to rise 4,000 feet in the air. In addition to hitting the Focke-Wulf assembly, bursts landed on the installations of the Spinnfaser Textile Mill, the Feka Factory (special machine tools), the Bahr Ludwig Paper Factory, and the Salzman Factory (linen, sailcloth, and cotton weaving). Estimate of the damage caused by the 4th Wing was difficult due to the intense smoke over the target, but hits were seen on a component erecting shop and a machine shop, while a storage building was gutted. The blast effect was noticeable over the entire area. Perhaps owing to a deep penetration by P-47' s to cover the withdrawal from the area, losses were no more than expected. Twelve bombers went down and claims of 48-13-32 were made.

Although German single-engine fighter production reportedly reached 810 planes per month in July, the beginning of the second phase of the CBO marked the first time a really concentrated effort was made to reduce German aircraft expansion. During the next month, the output of Focke-Wulf and Messerschmitt fighters was to fall to 665, thereby justifying the conclusion that "the major effect of the bombing program has been not so much to force production below previous levels as to halt in its tracks an immense fighter aircraft expansion program."

In addition, the Fighter and Bomber Commands listed in their records 575 enemy planes as shot down during the month. Despite a serious shortage of heavy bombers and crews to man them, operations showed a great increase over June. The bomb load of 4,103 tons on enemy targets was delivered in 1615 sorties at a cost of 113 planes, or a 7.3 percent loss out of planes reaching the objectives.

#

The first mission of August against German fighter production was remarkable for two reasons: it was a mission against a new target, and it was not conducted by the Eighth Air Force. The story of operation JUGGLER on 13 August brings the Ninth Air Force into POINTBLANK for the first time and also marks the first attack on the great Messerschmitt complex at Weiner Neustadt just south of Vienna.

The Ninth had been engaged in the North African campaign and had then taken part in the Sicilian invasion. For this campaign, the two B-24 groups, which constituted its heavy bombardment force, were augmented by the 93d, 44th, and 389th Groups (B-24) from the VIII Bomber Command. These five groups were diverted to prepare for TIDALWAVE, or the attack on the Ploesti oilfields. This famous mission was carried out on 1 August; immediately afterwards, the task force was ordered to prepare for a coordinated attack with the Eighth Air Force on Regensburg and Wiener Neustadt. This mission, known by the code name of JUGGLER, had been planned for some time. Behind the planning lay the growing concern of British and American authorities at the continued expansion of the Luftwaffe's fighter strength in the West, along with a resulting desire to strike at important centers of the air industry such as Regensburg and Wiener Neustadt that were still unacquainted with American precision bombing. Furthermore, both General Arnold and General Spaatz were anxious to bomb German industry from other bases than those in the United Kingdom. Both felt for some time that operations from Mediterranean bases against areas of the Reich were desirable and logical. Since most of the attacks on aircraft factories had been directed against Focke-Wulf centers, it was time to turn to the great Messerschmitt complexes, which had produced an estimated 570 Me-109's in July.

As originally planned, JUGGLER was a simultaneous attack on two centers: the Eighth was to assault Regensburg at the same time as the TIDAL-WAVE task force, or what was left of it, was striking north from the at Wiener Neustadt. For a while there was some chance that JUGGLER might be given a higher priority than TIDALWAVE, but since both Marshall and Arnold were opposed, it was finally decided to mount the Ploesti mission first, then run off the combined attack once repairs had been made and the crews had rested.

As previously indicated, the Rumanian objectives were attacked on 1 August and thereupon JUGGLER was set for 7 August. However, weather conditions over Northwestern Europe interfered with the Eighth's attack on Regensburg; after several postponements, it was decided to give up the idea of a coordinated attack and instead allow either force to stage its mission once conditions were favorable. As a result, the Ninth carried out its assignment on the 13th, four days before the Eighth could move. At 7 o'clock in the morning, 114 B-24's led by Brig. Gen. P. W. Timberlake took off from the Eighth's African bases and started on the long 1,200 mile trip to Austria. Despite two extra bomb bay tanks in each Liberator, the formations would not be able to return to their home bases, but they were to land at Tunisian fields for preliminary interrogations and refueling.

Although a large number of the bombers aborted—thirty-two returned to their bases before reaching the target and twenty-two others failed to bomb for mechanical or other reasons—the sixty-one Liberators that reached Wiener Neustadt gave a good account of themselves. Bursts covered the targets. Only one bomber was lost and two enemy planes were shot down. A photo reconnaissance revealed the extent of the injuries done to the installations. At the Wiener Neustadt works, two assembly shops out of four were badly damaged, several stores buildings were hit, and one large flight hangar was destroyed. Some of the bombs missed the Menschel Plant and fell in nearby fields, but one long store building received a direct hit and a workshop was one-third destroyed. Although the original estimate that Me-109 production at Wiener Neustadt had been cut fifty percent now seems little high, there is no doubt that considerable damage was inflicted on a duplex that hitherto had been immune to attacks. Because of this, and because it was the first strategic mission into the Reich from the Mediterranean, operation JUGGLER may be considered a history-making event in the development of the great air offensive against the Luftwaffe.

#

While the preparations for JUGGLER were underway, the Eighth was waiting for clearing weather. On 12 August, conditions had permitted a raid on Ruhr targets, but it was not until the 17th that a very deep penetration was possible. Therefore, the VIII Bomber Command had to content itself with short runs against airfields close to the Channel Coast on the 15th and 16th. On the first operation, 327 bombers were dispatched to attack the GAF bases at Vlissingen Poix, Amiens, Lille, and Vitry, France while the RAF and B-26's of the VIII Air Support Command carried out diversionary feints. Only two bombers were lost. The results of the bombings at Vlissingen, Lille and Poix were only fair, though far more successful elsewhere. At Amiens the entire airfield was blanketed with bursts, and hits were scored on hangars, workshops, barracks, and a runway. The entire northeast dispersal area was well covered with fragmentation bombs. Equally satisfactory bombings took place at Merville, France and Vitry. One interesting feature of this mission was an elaborate double feint that the 4th Wing carried out. Previously, the formations would make a diversion up the Channel toward the enemy coast and then proceed to the target. This drew the GAF into the air but when the feint was unmasked, the fighters would have spent much of their fuel. Becoming aware of this trick, the enemy had formed the habit of holding back his fighters and only releasing them once the bombers made their second turn toward the coast. On this mission, therefore, it was determined that the 4th Wing should make two threats toward the enemy coast before beginning the actual penetration of the enemy air. This plan worked successfully. At the second feint, the GAF reacted vigorously and some seventy fighters took to the air. However, they wasted their gasoline rushing out to meet the 4th Wing; by the time the real penetration was taking place, the German fighters were on the ground refueling. The fighter escort was unusually effective on this operation and won special praise from Brig. Gen. Frederick L. Anderson, Jr., commander of the Eighth's bombers.

Another new technique used on this significant mission was the employment of fragmentation and light GF bombs as the best combination for inflicting the maximum destruction on an airdrome. Gen. Spaatz had tried this tactic with considerable success in the Mediterranean theater, and it was found to work equally well in northwest Europe.

The next day the attack on the airfields continued. The 1st Wing went to Le Bourget and bombed with very good results, including some 600 bursts potholing the landing field and causing severe damage to repair shops, hangars, administration buildings, and barracks. The results of the 4th Wing's attack on Poix and Abbeville airdromes were considered fair. Both targets were attacked by a total of 236 bombers dropping 397.35 tons. Only four bombers were lost and claims of 29-3-11 were made. The build-up of fighter strength in the theater to 298 P-47's with 586 crews was beginning to make possible a more effective escort. Commenting on this mission, General Anderson wrote:

```
"It is felt that this operation is an excellent example of fighter-bomber
coordination. The 1st Wing penetrated enemy territory through an area
which is very heavily defended by fighters and reported only 59
encounters, with the loss of one a/c to enemy fighters. This number of
encounters is quite low, and it is evident that the fighter escort of
P-47's was effective."
```

#

By this time, the weather had improved to the extent that a deep penetration could be attempted; consequently, the Eighth planned to carry out the mission against Regensburg, which had originally been a part of the JUGGLER plan. Since the distance was great, the 4th Air Division assigned to the Regensburg attack was to continue across the Mediterranean and land at bases in north Africa. At the same time, the 1st Air Division was to attack the relatively closer target of Schweinfurt, the center of German ball-bearing manufacture. Three combat wings were assigned to the first task force, with two assigned to the second. To be able to mount major attacks against two important, heavily defended targets in the same day marked a milestone in the history of the Eighth Air Force. Nothing like this had been done before, and to carry out this double mission, the Bomber Command was strained to the limit of its resources. Out of the 613 B-17's and the 555 crews in the theater, 376 Flying Fortresses took the air on the morning of the 17th. A heavier commitment could have hardly been made.

Realizing that this double attack would probably cause a tremendous air battle, General Anderson and his staff laid their plans carefully. No fewer than eighteen squadrons of Thunderbolts from the VIII Fighter Command and sixteen squadrons of RAF Spitfires were to provide penetration support for the formations and withdrawal cover for the 1st division's bombers. Diversionary attacks were to be made by the medium bombers of the VIII on Bryas, France and Poix airfields, and RAF Typhoon bombers were to hit the airfields at Poix, Lille, and Woensdrecht, Holland, to hold down the German fighters in the area.

It had been originally ordered that the divisions should be dispatched ten minutes apart, but as the time for departure drew close, the unstable weather made this arrangement impossible. It was then decided to let the Schweinfurt task force take the air three and one-half hours later than the formations headed for Regensburg, thereby giving the fighter escort ample time to land, refuel, and get into the air again for the second force. Unsatisfactory as this arrangement may now seem, it must be remembered that bad weather had dogged the Eighth for some time, and on August 17th conditions along the entire route as well as over the targets were the best in two weeks. Dangerous as it was to dispatch the two task forces separately, it would have been more dangerous to send them without any escort, and the growing importance of the two targets did not permit an extended delay.

The mission took place against intense opposition. From Antwerp to the Alps the squadrons were under almost constant attack from about 200 German fighters drawn from all parts of the Reich, with one group coming into the fray as fast as another withdrew. Near Regensburg, twin-engine fighters with desert camouflage were seen. Some fighters were called in from Holland to the Rhineland, and every type of fighter the GAF possessed was thrown into the struggle. As the battle progressed and the bomber formations plowed deeper and deeper into Germany, the tension among the German fighter pilots mounted. Allied listeners intercepting German radio signals heard a strange medley of warnings, exclamations, and imprecations. Calls of "close up," "look out," "formation coming up behind," and "fighters to starboard" passed rapidly back and forth among the German planes. At 1636 hours, when the Thunderbolts and Spitfires entered the melee to cover the retiring 1st Division, the combat reached its height. Claims of strikes and kills were heard over the German radio, mingled with cries of "parachute, ha, down you go you dog," and after almost half an hour's combat, a final gasp of "Herr Gott Sakramant." By 1700 it was over.

The bombing was successful, but at the heaviest cost the Eighth Air force had suffered. Out of the 308 bombers which attacked the targets, 60 were shot down, a loss of 19 percent of the attacking force; 36 had gone down at Schweinfurt; and 24 fell at Regensburg; however, the damage inflicted had been great. At Schweinfurt, the three roller bearing factories were hit several times. In the Kugelfischer fuel injection plant, four large machine shops and a storage building were partly destroyed and an office building was gutted. At the Vereinigte Kugellager Fabrike Werke I, one unidentified building was severely damaged; at Werke II, some machine shops were badly injured.

At Regensburg the results were even better. Within the target area sixty-two installations were damaged and the number seriously damaged or destroyed came to thirteen workshops, five office buildings, nineteen unidentified structures, and seventeen others, including a final assembly shop, a gun-testing range, three light-metals buildings, a hangar for engine installations, and ten living quarters. Reconnaissance photos showed fifty-one single-engine aircraft on the field of which thirty-seven were probably destroyed or damaged. Total claims for destroyed, probably destroyed, and damaged aircraft were set at the very high figures of 290-38-99. Even assuming these are probably extreme, there can be little doubt that the Luftwaffe paid a steep price for the afternoon's entertainment.

#

After this great effort, the VIII Bomber Command relaxed while missions were carried out against Luftwaffe airfields and ground installations. Weather badly hampered a mission against Dutch and Belgium fields on the 19th, which amounted to little. On the 24th, Villacoublay was attacked with excellent results, and Bordeaux, Evreux, and Conches were hit less successfully. The attack on Bordeaux was made by the units of the Regensburg task force returning from their shuttle trip to North Africa; a cloud over the city prevented accurate use of the bombsights and the results were only fair. Three days later the 1st Division sent 224 aircraft to attack more aeronautical facilities in France. Although thirty-seven planes failed to bomb, the results were considered excellent, with only four bombers lost. On the last day of the month, finding primary and secondary targets covered by cloud, a force of 106 bombers assailed the Amiens airdrome as a target of opportunity. The results were excellent: five dense concentrations covered the target with hits on all the main installations, and some bursts on a railroad marshalling yard near the airfield.

In the war against the Luftwaffe, August must be recorded as one of the more successful months. Although the bomb tonnage was a little lower than July's, this was overshadowed by the fact that the Air Ministry estimates showed a considerable drop in GAF production. Instead of advancing still further toward the 1,000-plane-a-month goal, the output of Messerschmitt and Focke-Wulf fighters fell from a high of 810 to 665 during August. For the first time since the CBO was initiated, Me-109 centers were attacked successfully, and the production of this fighter was cut from 570 to 435 during the month.

In spite of heavy casualties on the Regensburg-Schweinfurt operation, total losses for August were slightly less than July, dropping from 7.3 to 7.0 percent of the planes actually attacking. The operations against airfields during the last week of August were connected with an elaborate plan—operation STARKEY. This was a combined RAF-AAF operation designed to force the Luftwaffe to commit a large part of its forces to battles of attrition so the maximum number of enemy planes could be destroyed in the air and on the ground. The core of the GAF opposition to the daylight raids was the some 680 fighters stationed in northwest Germany and Holland, and approximately 170 fighters based around Lille, Poix, and the Beaumont-le-Roger farther south. The bombing of these fields in July and August tended to force the Luftwaffe back from the coast, and the fields in northern France may have been evacuated before the commencement of STARKEY. At any rate, it was hoped that the elaborate maneuvers planned as a part of the operation would force the GAF "to stick its neck out" and enable the

Allies to win the air superiority so important to further land and air movements against the Continent.

The plan was divided into 3 phases: (1) the preliminary phase from 16 to 24 August, (2) the preparatory phase from 25 August to 8 September, and (3) a culminating phase on 8-9 September, when with the cooperation of naval units, an "invasion" of the Continent would be simulated from British ports. It was believed that this ruse would bring on a large-scale air battle. The organization responsible for RAF participation in STARKEY was No. 11 Group, which was strongly reinforced by squadrons from Nos. 10, 12, and 13 Groups' being absorbed into the No. 11 Group Sector. Also temporary operational control of squadrons from 83 and 84 Groups was given to No. 11; medium bombers (No. 2 Group) and the Coastal Commands antishipping Beaufighters were likewise assigned to the air command for the operation. For the D-Day ruse, additional reinforcements were to come from Nos. 10 and 12 groups. The AAF participation was largely limited to the medium bombers of the VIII with whatever assistance the strict priorities of the VIII Bomber Command and the weather would permit. As it later turned out, weather was far more of a problem than priorities or the Luftwaffe.

During the preliminary phase, action centered largely against enemy airfields. A total of twenty-one attacks were made and forty-five enemy aircraft destroyed at a cost of twenty-three. The enemy reaction to the opening phase of STARKEY was cautious, and bad weather slowed down the tempo of attacks. During the big operation against Regensburg and Schweinfurt, the STARKEY task forces ran diversionary raids against Luftwaffe bases, as previously noted, and shot down fifteen German planes against a loss of three. All together 6,000 fighter and bomber sorties were flown during the nine days of this phase.

The preparatory phase which began 25 August was intended to speed up operations with blows against airfields, industrial targets, and military installations in and related to the Pas de Calais area; however, the weather seriously interfered. Of the forty-two operations planned, fourteen were canceled outright, eleven abandoned, and three seriously curtailed, leaving only fifteen which were flown as planned. As actually carried out, the preparatory phase was divided into two sub-periods: (1) from 25 August to 3 September; and (2) from 4 to 8 September. During the first sub-period, twenty attacks were made on airfields, with the heaviest blows being struck against Beaumont-le-Roger, Tricqueville, Poix, and Amiens. Since photo reconnaissance revealed that the enemy was basing fighters at Camorai, Beuvais, and Lille/Nord, the last two were attacked. Toward the later part of this phase the heavy bombers of the VIII Bomber Command contributed to the plan by attacking two air fields on 2 September, with six more the following day. This last bomber sweep of airfields was a considerable mission involving 296 bombers dropping 2736 x 500-1b. GF bombs. Nine planes were lost and claims were relatively modest being only 26-5-10. The reaction of the GAF continued to be cautious, to say the least.

Beginning with the 4th, the emphasis of the bombers was shifted to marshalling yards, which were presumed to affect the area of the supposed landings. On this day the GAF showed a slight tendency to react and lost planes as a result. It was believed the Germans had used long-range bombers for laying mines in the channel on the night of 3-4 September. When the Royal Navy conducted a mine sweep, this produced a German air reconnaissance – the first one carried out during STARKEY. With overcast conditions complicating the bombing of Germany, a part of a formation of Fortresses came to the assistance of the STARKEY operations and bombed additional airfields in France on 6 September. Because of clouds, the results were unobserved. The next day three operations were run off against air depots, aeronautical stations and other airfields.

Meanwhile, during several weeks prior to the final phase of STARKEY, large bodies of troops had been moved into the southeast counties of England, and motor transport vehicles and antiaircraft personnel began to assemble near assault craft designed to simulate the "bridgehead" formations of an invading Army. Between Southampton and The Thames estuary large numbers of ships began to appear at various anchorages and ports. As the last phase began, the air challenge was to silence the German long-range guns on the French coast that might have thrown the proposed operation into considerable hazard; consequently, RAF and AAF fighters and medium bombers were to neutralize these gun positions. Although the last phase was to start during the night of 7-September, weather forced a postponement until the night of 9 September.

The first attacks of the final phase were made by bombers against seven battery positions while two fighter-bombers attacked beach defenses. These attacks were successful and almost unopposed. At about 0700 hours, the naval assault force, under an umbrella of planes, set out from Dungeness and swept down the Channel for Le Touquet, France. About an hour later, the Eighth Air Force unleashed a heavy simultaneous attack against the seven principal airdromes in northwest France. A total of 377 bombers participated in the raids. Only two were lost and since the Luftwaffe's opposition was light, claims were only 16-2-9. While this was going on, the convoy proceeded down the Channel till 0900 when the British laid a smoke screen; under cover of this, the fleet turned about and landed at Dungeness near 1100. The enemy air reaction to the naval maneuvers was nil.

In summing up the results of this long, carefully planned operation, the official report made it quite clear that all attempts at deception had failed. The enemy was never deceived into thinking that a serious landing was attempted; consequently, it made no attempt to use his fighters against our land or sea operations. Once again it was made clear that only deep penetrations to vital industrial targets would bring the Luftwaffe out in force. Although the Germans did reinforce their fighters in the Beauvais and Lille areas, these measures were mainly precautionary and did not cause any fundamental change in their disposition of fighters. In the words of the final report:

"It is beyond the scope of this report to consider the reasons why the enemy appreciated that a full scale landing was not intended. It is suggested, however, that this may have been due either to his having had information that the extent of the Army participation in this operation amounted to little more than an administrative exercise …or else to a firm conviction that there could be no serious threat of invasion from this Country at the present time. The enemy's almost complete lack of overland reconnaissance, both prior to and during this Operation lends colour to either of these hypotheses."

In the vernacular, STARKEY was a flop.

#

After a pause of a week, the offensive against German airfields resumed. On the 15th, four task forces were dispatched to attack German industrial targets in France and certain airdromes. Ninety-three bombers of the 1st Division struck at the aircraft storage and repair depot at Romilly-sur-Seine with excellent results, and the 2d Division bombed the Chartres airfield as a last-resort target. The following day 295 bombers were dispatched in a sweep of targets from Brittany to the Bay of Biscay. Among the objectives were the Nantes/ Chateau Bougon airfield and GAF installations at La Rochelle/Laleu and Cognac/Chateubernard. Claims were 44-5-13 at a cost of eleven heavy bombers. Again on the 23d the Forts were out, this time against certain Breton airfields. Vannes/Meucon was bombed by fifty-five planes with good results, and Rennes/St. Jacques was hit by nineteen with only fair results. The last counter-air force operation of the month took place on the 26th when forty bombers blanketed the Reims/Champagne airfield with GP and incendiary bombs, causing much damage.

September was a month of greatly increased operations. A total of 2,085 bomber sorties reached their targets with a relatively low loss of 4.7 percent of the attacking planes. Bomb tonnage reached a new high of 5743 tons for the month. On the other hand, claims were considerably lower, with 303 destroyed as compared to the 457 for the previous month. This is probably because so many of the missions were against relatively undefended coastal airfields. It is also probable that the Luftwaffe was beginning to follow a policy of conserving his fighters and did not wish to commit its forces to battle unless the stakes were high.

At the same time, a good many of the missions of September were relatively small affairs; yet the build-up of strength in the theater was greater than ever before. There were 749 heavy bombers with 871 crews and 422 fighters with 869 crews. That the missions were flown with relatively small numbers of bombers troubled General Arnold who, on 25 September, cabled Gen. Ira G. Eaker, commander of the Eighth Air Force: "We obviously must send the maximum number of airplanes against targets within Germany. I know you will agree that the minimum number must be kept on the ground at our bases or in reserve." He went on to say he was under constant pressure to explain why we did not use massive flights of planes since we now had enough to put 500 in the air. The very next day, Arnold again cabled to get the facts about German aircraft production, especially the effects of the August bombings.

General Eaker's reply was reassuring. He believed the Eighth's raids had materially reduced the German single-engine plane production and stated "an educated guess indicates further reduction in Me-109 production for September." He thought that shifts in location plus the withdrawal of planes from the Eastern front might offset the destruction of the older plants; thus, an increase of strength was probably to be expected in the Mediterranean area. Regardless, he believed the new units would be made up of green crews and that in any event shifting airplanes merely masked the true decline in the German fighter forces.

A few days later, after a raid of 2 October on Emden with exceptionally light losses, he was able to cable General Arnold that the weak German fighter attacks on our formations stemmed from a shortage of single-engine fighters caused by our attacks on German fighter factories.

The Emden raid was followed on 4 October by an extensive mission involving four task forces made up of 361 bombers. One formation of 38 B-17's attacked the St. Dizier/Robinson airfield in France as a last-resort target, but little damage was done. Bombers from the 1st Division attacked the Vereinigte Deutsche Metall Werke at Frankfort. This plant produced more than fifty percent of the metal propellers used by GAF fighters, reconnaissance planes and bombers. A photo reconnaissance taken a few hours after the raid showed the plant still burning, and between one-half and one-third destroyed. This mission marked the debut of the B-24H bomber which, according to General Eaker, "gave a good account of itself in its first combat." From all the forces attacking, sixteen heavy bombers were lost. The preliminary claims were 56-24-22, but these were later re-evaluated and became 87-24-47.

On the 8th the heaviest attack up to that time was carried out against Germany. Four air task forces, involving 399 Fortresses and Liberators, went out against various targets. One force of 53 B-17's dropped 180 x 500-1b. GP and 720 x 100-1b. IB bombs on the Focke-Wulf airframe plant at Bremen. Unfortunately the bombing was not good this time. The strike photos showed two possible hits with most of the bombs falling outside the target area. Claims for all the task forces reached the very high figure of 167-22-35 with the heavy loss of thirty bombers. However, an RAF raid in the same area that night sustained a loss of three bombers, showing the value of cooperative missions.

The story of the 113th operation on 9 October is tersely and neatly summed up in the Narrative of Operations:

```
"Five air task forces of Fortresses and Liberators made the deepest
penetration into Germany since the beginning of operations by VIII Bomber
Command to successfully attack important naval and industrial targets in
eastern Germany. Bombing results were excellent ...28 heavy bombers failed
to return and claims against are 122-29-61."
```

The 1st Division sent 115 B-17's to bomb the Arado plant at Anklam, Germany, a major producer of FW-190 component parts assembled at Tutow. The results were excellent in spite of the loss of fifteen big planes. Concentrations of bursts covered the entire factory and every major unit of the plant sustained damage.

The 3d Division dispatched 100 B-17's against the important FW-190 assembly plant at Marienburg, which was then supposed to have inherited most of the functions previously carried out at Bremen. This raid was one of the most effective of the year. All but four of the dispatched planes attacked the target from the relatively low altitude of 11,000 to 13,500 feet, yet only two of the Fortresses were lost. The plant was practically destroyed with hits on all major units except one assembly shop at the north end. As the planes departed, the entire target was a mass of smoke and flame; three hours later, the fires were still so intense that photo reconnaissance was impossible.

The day following the mission, General Eaker cabled General Arnold the following message:

```
"Have just seen first photos of yesterdays attacks; most encouraging.
Fighter factory Marienburg undoubtedly destroyed.It will be a better
example of pin point bombing...a better concentration than Regensburg.
Looks like a perfect job. Fighter factory at Anklam received excellent
concentration and principal buildings burning ...Believe you will find
October 9th a day to remember in air war. Prime Minister is sending
message to crews."
```

Two years later when Hermann Goering was being interrogated as to the effects of our bombing offensive, the August raids on Regensburg and

Wiener Neustadt and the October raid on Marienburg still remained in his mind as among our most successful efforts.

#

Five days later, the Eighth achieved another outstanding mission with its follow-up attack on Schweinfurt. As previously described in this chapter, Schweinfurt had been successfully bombed on 17 August. By this time, it was assumed that repairs were nearly completed and the target was ready for a follow-up attack. Furthermore, it had been observed that deep penetrations against vital objectives always produced a violent Luftwaffe reaction, and it was hoped that in defense of this important ball-bearing plant, the GAF would commit large forces to the air battle.

These expectations were fulfilled. The 291 bombers of the task moved steadily across northern Europe, the German fighters were assembling, waiting for the moment when the escorts would turn back and leave the big planes open to attack. A formation of twenty-nine bombers flew a diversion in the direction of Emden. As the groups passed over the Aachen-Duren area, the fighter escort left, and the first German attack squadrons dived into the bomber formations. The first wave of bombers was hardest hit. Approximately 300 enemy planes attacked the squadrons using a combination of single-engine fighters coordinated with twin-engine rocket-firing airplanes. The attacks were very effective; out of this first wave, 45 bombers were lost and only 101 were able to reach the target. In spite of this fierce opposition, a combination of improving weather, and a clever feint away from the target that threw off the swarms of German aircraft, enabled the two attacking formations to bomb with considerable success. The main installations were hit, and many fires were burning when the bombers left the area.

In the V L F Works I, all the main buildings in the southwest end were gutted by fire while seven buildings in V L F Works II were more than half destroyed. The Deutsche Star Rugelhalter plant, which manufactured ball-bearing cages, the storage buildings were completely destroyed and the machine shops were damaged. According to the Narrative of Operations of the Bomber Command, seventy-five percent of Schweinfurt's productive capacity was wiped out. The destruction of sixty bombers marked this operation as one of the costliest missions carried out, but this loss was partially offset by the very large preliminary claims of 176-27-89; these were later supported by the final evaluation.

In spite of heavy losses, it was soon recognized that the Schweinfurt raid of fourteen October was an outstanding mission. General Arnold cabled that he was particularly gratified that morale and enthusiasm were high. "Convey this message to your command," he wrote Eaker, "... the cornered wolf fights hardest and .. the German Air Force has been driven into its last corner." Secretary of War Stimson sent his "heartiest congratulations and deep admiration ...to all ranks of the Eighth Air Force." General George Marshall stated that he was "tremendously impressed with the apparent complete destruction of the Schweinfurt Ball Bearing Plant," which, he believed, would have an effect on the general German position comparable to that of the Ploesti mission.

The air battle of Schweinfurt was the last counter-air force operation of a month which, according to Eighth Air Force claims, was the most costly yet endured by the Luftwaffe. In all, 870 enemy aircraft were destroyed (Bomber Command claims alone came to 791-80-71), but American losses were far from light. In fact, the 186 heavy bombers destroyed constituted 9.7 percent of the attacking forces, a term that does not include forces dispatched but only those that reached the target area, and made October's air operations the most costly of the European war. The actual monthly loss of bombers was destined to go much higher—April of 1944 it would reach 420 —but at no time would the percentage of loss come to October's figure. From this time onward, the build-up of American bomber and fighter strength would always keep well ahead of attrition.

Was the GAF defeated? Could it continue to withstand such heavy pressure? General Arnold, at least, was hopeful that the end of serious resistance in the air could not be long deferred. "From my viewpoint," he cabled Eaker, "it appears that the last months operations on all fronts may indicate that the German Air Force is on the verge of collapse. Frantic employment of all types of defensive aircraft may mean the Luftwaffe is staving off a crisis." In reply, General Eaker stated that he saw no definite indication of collapse, but much evidence of strain. Our bombing would cut German single-engine fighter production thirty-five to forty percent by the end of

November, and reserves were very low. On the whole his outlook was very optimistic: "It can be stated with certainty that the completion of operations as scheduled will produce the desired result."

#

With the close of October, the second stage of the CBO came to an end. As originally scheduled, it called for a theater strength of 1,192 planes providing an average striking force of 450. The main emphasis of attacks in the plan was to be against the German aircraft industry and within a 400 mile radius of the coast.

As executed, this phase of the bombing plan surpassed the schedule though at other times it was considered behind. In the sense of the Regensburg missions the 400 radius was considerably exceeded, yet a large number of missions had been near the Channel coast. German aircraft factories had been hit but since German fighters often interfered with the missions, a great many formations had to be content bombing German-held aerodromes in northern France. Then, too, a large number of heavy and medium bombers had been diverted from vital targets to the unsuccessful STARKEY operation.

Perhaps the greatest deviation from schedule was the build-up of planes in England: the 799 bombers present in the United Kingdom (with units) were well under the 1,192 planes the second phase requested. As a result, none of the operations came near the 450-plane formations, which many hoped would be the size of the average raid for July-October.

In pointing out where the plan fell short of its creators expectations, it is only fair to state that the many of the obstacles encountered could not have possibly been foreseen when the air offensive against Germany was being planned. What some of these problems were and how they were met will be the subject of the next chapter. Suffice it to say, these caused major problems for the Eighth and the frustrated Generals Eaker and Arnold.

A FRESH CREW ARRIVES WITH A NEW BOMBER. DURING THE EARLY MONTHS OF 1944, AS MANY AS 200 NEW CREWS LIKE THIS WERE REQUIRED TO SIMPLY KEEP UP WITH LOSES.

THE FW-190.

DISCIPLINED FLYING WAS A NECESSITY. WITH TIGHT FORMATIONS
THE MAXIMUM AVAILABLE FIREPOWER WAS AIMED OUT TOWARDS THE
ENEMY.THESE B-17S ARE SEEN WITH A P-38 LIGHTENING [UPPER RIGHT].

THE WAIST GUNNER ON A B-17. COLD AIR SWIRLED THROUGH THE FUSELAGE OF OUR BOMBERS
GUNNERS WORE ARCTIC FLIGHT SUITS WITH ELECTRICAL HEATERS BUT FROSTBITE WAS AN
EARLY PROBLEM.MISSIONS WERE FLOWN AT ALTITUDES OF 25,000 FEET OR HIGHER.

THE P-51 MUSTANG. LONG RANGE ESCORT FIGHTERS WERE INTRODUCED LATE IN THE AIR WAR BUT QUICKLY SLOWED THE LOSSES.

[LEFT]
MASCOTS AND NOSE ART PROVIDED A LITTLE RELIEF FROM THE STRESS OF AIR WAR.

52110 A.C.

THE DOUBLE-MISSION FLOWN BY THE USAAF ON AUGUST 17, 1943 CAME
ABOUT ONLY THROUGH HEAVY BOMBER LOSSES. THE TARGETS-- FIGHTER
PLANTS AT REGENSBURG AND THE BALL BEARING PLANTS AT
SCHWEINFURT. IT WOULD BE ONE OF THE BLOODIEST DAYS IN THE AIR
WAR. A CLOSE INSPECTION OF THIS PHOTO REVEALS A CREWMAN
BAILING OUT THROUGH THE TOPHATCH JUST BEHIND THE COCKPIT.

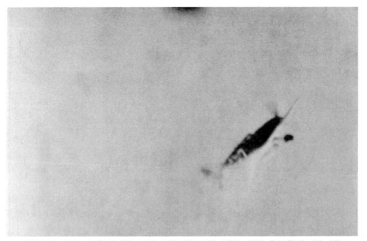

A GERMAN AIR FORCE ME-109 CAUGHT IN THE GUN SIGHTS OF AN
AMERICAN FIGHTER.

A P-47 THUNDERBOLT JUMPS IN THE TAIL OF A GERMAN ME-110. THIS UNUSUAL
VIEW IS THROUGH THE GUN CAMERA OF A SECOND P-47 IN THE PURSUIT.

THIS B-17 WAS BRUTALLY DECAPITATED. THE GERMANS FIRED ROCKETS
INTO FORMATIONS, DROPPED MORTAR BOMBS DOWN ON FORMATIONS AND IN
FRUSTRATION WOULD SIMPLY RAM THE BOMBERS.

THE WHITE FLASHES ARE SHELLS HITTING THIS GERMAN FIGHTER
DURING A DOGFIGHT.

STRAFING A GERMAN AIRFIELD. IN ADDITION TO TRADITIONAL
FIGHTER BASES, AIR FIELDS WERE OFTEN "FIELDS," THAT IS LARGE
OPEN SPACES WITH OR WITHOUT AN IMPROVED RUNWAY.

A P-47 THUNDERBOLT STRAFES. ATTACKING GERMAN AIR FIELDS WAS
ONE OF THE DECISIVE CHANGES INSTITUTED BY SPAATZ AND
DOOLITTLE.

A B-24 SPIRALS OVER AFTER LOSING THE LEFT WING. OUT OF CONTROL
BOMBERS WERE A TERRIFYING SIGHT AND OFTEN FLIPPED INTO ANOTHER
AIRPLANE IN THE FORMATION.

FLAX TOWERS SUCH AS THIS ONE DOTTED THE APPROACHES TO MAJOR
GERMAN CITIES. A P-47 ATTACKS.

DEATH AT 25,000 FEET. PERHAPS A GERMAN SHELL HIT THE BOMB LOAD;
PERHAPS A GERMAN ROCKET FOUND ITS MARK. AIR WARFARE WAS AS
SUDDEN AS IT WAS UNFORGIVING. LITTLE MATCHED THE HORROR OF
PLUNGING TENS OF THOUSANDS OF FEET TO THE GROUND.

[THREE-SHOT SEQUENCE.] GUN CAMERA FOOTAGE OF AN ATTACK ON A GERMAN ME-110.

[THREE SHOT SEQUENCE.] ALTHOUGH AMERICA WAS LATE ENTERING
THE WAR, OUR PILOTS HAD BETTER TRAINING AND A SUPERIOR
FIGHTER IN THE P-51.

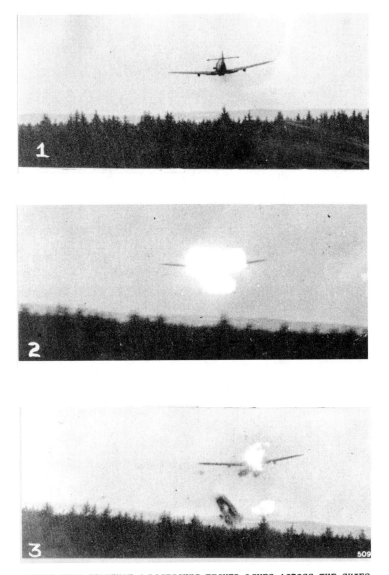

[THREE SHOT SEQUENCE.] DOGFIGHTS ETCHED LINES ACROSS THE SKIES
AND DOWN TO THE DECK. THIS GERMAN FIGHTER IS BLOWN APART MERE
FEET ABOVE THE GROUND.

IT APPEARS THAT THIS B-17 WAS HIT BY THE BOMBS RELEASED BY
ANOTHER BOMBER AND WHILE THAT DID HAPPEN IT WAS RARE. WHATEVER
THE STORY, THE FUSELAGE HAS ALL BUT DISINTEGRATED LEAVING A
TRAIL OF DEBRIS FOR OTHERS TO AVOID.

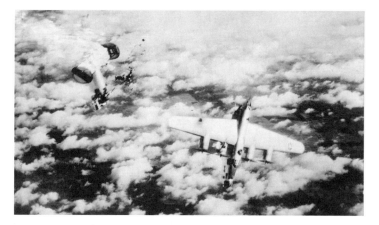

A B-24 LIBERATOR WITH ITS TAIL SECTION SHOT OFF. THIS BOMBER
WILL PITCH-POLE FORWARD AND DOWN PRESSING THE CREWMEN AGAINST
THE INTERIOR OF THE FUSELAGE WITH NEARLY UNBREAKABLE G-FORCES.

PERHAPS MORE THAN ANY PHOTO, THIS WAS THE SIGNATURE IMAGE OF
THE AIR WAR OVER GERMANY. REPRODUCED BY THE DEPARTMENT OF
DEFENSE ON THE 50TH ANNIVERSARY OF VE DAY, THIS B-17 HAS BEEN
SO THOROUGHLY SHOT UP THAT ITS RIGHT WING HAS SEPARATED AND
HALF OF ITS TAIL SECTION HAS BEEN BLOWN APART.

20MM CANNON FIRE DEVASTATED AMERICAN BOMBERS AS SEEN IN THIS
PHOTO OF A B-17. BOMBERS THAT FELL OUT OF FORMATIONS WERE
CALLED "CRIPPLES."

ASYMMETRICAL LIFT CAUSED BY THE SHEARED RIGHT WING AND FORCED
THIS B-17 INTO A SPIRALING SPIN.

D-DAY. INCREDIBLY, PHOTO JOURNALISTS ACCOMPANIED THE FIRST WAVE HOWEVER THERE ARE FEW SURVIVING IMAGES OF THE ACTUAL INVASION. ONE PHOTO JOURNALIST OVER PROCESSED HIS NEGATIVES AND DESTROYED SEVERAL ROLLS OF PRICELESS IMAGES. THE SIGNAL CORPS IMAGE WAS TAKEN DURING THE FIRST HOUR OF THE INVASION AND WAS TRANSMITTED ELECTRONICALLY THUS THE VISIBLE STREAKS IN THE PHOTO.

MORE THAN 600 B-17S AND B-24S ARE VISIBLE IN THIS PICTURE.
THIS REPRESENTS THE SIZE OF A "MAXIMUM EFFORT" MISSION AGAINST
GERMANY. THE LARGEST BOMBER MISSIONS SAW MORE THAN 1,000
AIRPLANES TAKE WING.

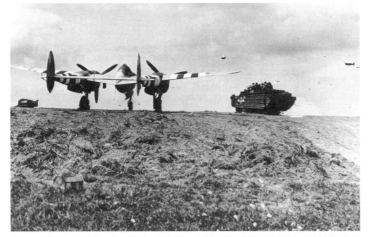

AIR FIELDS WERE QUICKLY CARVED OUT OF THE FIELDS ABOVE THE
D-DAY BEACHES. A P-38 GETS A WELCOME RESPITE DAYS AFTER THE
LANDINGS.

HAP ARNOLD AND OMAR BRADLEY WALK THE D-DAY BEACHES ON D+6. THE
RELIEF ON THEIR FACES SPEAKS VOLUMES ABOUT THE TRIUMPH OF OF
THE US ARMY AIR FORCES OVER THE LUFTWAFFE AND THE VICTORY THAT
WAS D-DAY.

3

MAINTAINING THE PRESSURE ON THE GAF

For convenience, the last chapter dealt almost entirely with the early operations of the POINTBLANK program, the targeting of German aircraft manufacturing and forward airfields; therefore, it was necessary to omit an account of some of the problems the Eighth Air Force faced in trying to hold to the established plan of operations. Now is the time to consider them. Briefly, there were three major factors that affected the progress of the attack on the Luftwaffe during 1943: (1) the diversion of men and equipment from the Eighth to other air organizations; (2) the slow build-up of American air power in the theater; and (3) the terribly high cost of the air offensive in terms of lives lost and bombers destroyed or damaged.

From the very beginning, the Eighth was called upon to contribute to the build-up of other air forces while it was still trying to get its own organization established and operating. Shortly after the Eighth arrived in England, the North African invasion was decided; many of the bombers and material, which were to arrive in the British Isles for the Eighth, had to be transferred to the Twelfth Air Force. The extent to which this held back operations was undoubtedly great, and the effects were felt for many months to come. By as late as June 1943, there were only 582 heavy bombers on hand with units in the VIII Bomber Command. Unsurprisingly, tensions between the various American commands in the two theaters were not rising,

Then, in spite of the fact that the Combined Bombing Offensive required 944 bombers to be in the theater by mid-1943, the Eighth was called upon to make another diversion. It was to send three B-24 groups to reinforce the Ninth Air Force for TIDALWAVE (Ploesti) and JUGGLER (Regensburg-Schweinfurt). As a result, between 26 June and 2 July, the 44th, 93d, and 389th groups were dispatched; the first two were old, experienced units, the 389th new and untried. Added to the earlier diversion of planes, this seemed to the straw that broke the camel's back. General Ira Eaker, Commander of the Eight Air Force, and General Jacob Devers, Commander of U.S. Army Forces in Europe, voiced vigorous complaints over this latest diversion. They urged for the groups to be used only for the Ploesti mission and then returned to England, since their loss reduced the bomber strength by one-fifth. However, the uses for heavy bombers were legion, and it proved difficult to get them back. The three groups flew in support of Operation HUSKY, the invasion of Sicily, from 2 to 19 July, and then were assigned to TIDALWAVE with JUGGLER presumably to follow. At this point, Eaker and Devers, assisted by Air Marshall Sir Charles Portal, attempted to give JUGGLER top priority over the Ploesti mission. They felt the GAF fighter factories were of "paramount and highest priority" and that such targets should have precedence over all others. At the same time, they again urged that the B-24's be returned to the Eighth as soon as possible.

This time the argument went all the way to the top. General of the Army George C. Marshall and General of the Army Air Force Henry "Hap" Arnold were asked to intervene. Neither wanted to see TIDALWAVE hampered in any way, but they asked General Dwight D. Eisenhower for his opinion, as well as that of British Air Marshall Arthur William Tedder and General Carl A. "Tooey" Spaatz, Commander of the Army Air Force Operation in Europe, on 19 July. Eisenhower, then Commanding General of the European Theatre of Operations and Supreme Commander Allied Expeditionary Force North Africa, replied with a compromise—of sorts. Like Marshall and Arnold, he did not want to abandon TIDALWAVE, especially with all the preparations involved. Since he believed greater losses might be expected from the Rumanian raid, he suggested JUGGLER come first since it would be the easier. While he appreciated General Eaker's desire to get his groups back, he felt some things were more important, such as follow-up raids on Ploesti. The question was finally brought before the Combined Chiefs of Staff and on the 23d, they cabled their decision to Eisenhower: TIDALWAVE was to have first priority, but the attack on the fighter factories was to take place as soon as arrangements could be made with the Eighth Air Force.

This issue was now settled, but while the three groups were in North Africa preparing for the attacks on Ploesti and Wiener Neustadt, a new demand was made for the Eighth's bombers. The Sicilian campaign was in full swing, and there was a great need for all available air power. Consequently, General Eisenhower requested four heavy bombardment groups from the Eighth Air Force. General Marshall forwarded this request on to General Devers who objected strongly. The coming period was highly important, as it was the phase of the CBO in which the GAF production was marked for destruction. Devers felt that the Eighth had at last reached a size where effective coordination with the RAF would be possible. In addition, he cited the successful raids on submarine installations and warned the bombers could not operate outside their own theater at the maximum efficiency. For these reasons he urged Marshall not to divert the Eighth from its official task. Evidently this appeal had some effect, for the Chief of Staff suggested to both Devers and Eisenhower that perhaps medium bombers could be substituted for the heavy groups. To this suggestion, Devers voiced similar objections, adding that the mediums had special commitments to STARKEY, which made it desirable to keep them in the theater. The Combined Chiefs of Staff again terminated this argument in a decision favorable to the air strategists and the CBO, and General Eisenhower's request was disapproved.

So far the Eighth, with the backing of General Devers, had been able to hold its remaining forces together for the POINTBLANK offensive. However, owing to the heavy losses at Ploesti, General Arnold agreed that some additional B-24's would have to be furnished General Lewis Brereton Commander of the Ninth Air Force for JUGGLER. On 5 August, Devers cabled Washington that he was sending six or possibly seven B-24's and crews to the Ninth.

With the successful conclusion of JUGGLER, another struggle began over the much sought-after B-24 groups. Once more Eisenhower asked for them, and Devers opposed cabling Generals Arnold and Marshall that if the groups were returned by 20 August, then they could accomplish the destruction of four to eight aircraft factories or aircraft engine plants in August or September. "Any delay now," he stated, "will jeopardize the success of the entire bomber offensive." Also, more B-24's were arriving in England from the United States, and the presence of the experienced groups in the theater was essential due to the training and morale factors involved. After several exchanges of cables, the Combined Chiefs of Staff reached a decision by 19 August; in a cable of that date, General Eisenhower referred to their decision to return the B-24's to General Eaker.

But this was not the last of the competition for the three groups whose control must have been rapidly assuming the proportions of a major headache for all concerned. On 15 September, General Eisenhower returned to the subject, again making a strong request for their services. This time the tactical situation was greatly in his favor. On the 9th, the Allies had made a very precarious landing at Salerno. The beach head held, but a heavy German counterattack had been launched on the 11th—and not till the 15th was there any assurance that the position could be maintained. However, the situation was still critical; Eisenhower assured the War Department that if assigned to him, the Liberator groups would be used on daily missions to upset communications between the north and south enemy concentrations. Upon receiving Eisenhower's cable, the Joint Chiefs of Staff agreed to lend him the B-24's for a short period, provided British concurrence could be obtained. This was soon given and on the 16th, Devers was able to report that the 93d, 389th, and 44th were to be sent, making a total of 87 aircraft and 108 combat crews. Thus, the Eighth again lost the use of practically all its experienced B-24 crews and their planes. However, it was evident that the arguments of General Devers had made an impression on the War Department for General Marshall made it clear that the groups were to be returned to England as soon as possible. On the 22 of September he cabled Eisenhower that the groups were sent to him as an emergency measure, and that the bomber offensive from England was weakened at a critical time. Pointing out there was considerable opposition, he concluded:

"I hope that you will see your way clear to release them very soon." This request was promptly complied; the planes were released on 24 September and shortly after returned to England.

It is probably useless to argue the question of what these three groups would have done had they been able to remain in England during July, August and September. However, it might be pointed out that during the first two months, the theater strength was low, and it seems very likely that their absence had something to with the decreased tonnage and claims for August. Important as was the POINTBLANK offensive, it had to compete with other high-ranking priorities, and it did not always succeed in holding its own. However, it is significant that after September 1943, the heavy-bomber forces in England were not raided again by other theaters. It is true that the medium bombers of the 3d Wing later became the nucleus for the IX Bomber Command which was organized in October, and it is also true that in November some heavy groups in the United States were switched from the Eighth to the Fifteenth. But the B-17's and B-24's in the theater were henceforth able to turn their undivided attention to the bombing program planned for them.

#

Another serious problem affecting the success of operations was a shortage in replacement crews. The situation became critical in June. Following the mission of the 13th against Kiel, Germany, in which losses were heavy, General Eaker cabled General Arnold: "it is now perfectly obvious we are going to have a tough battle." He was gravely concerned over the flow of replacement crews and felt that the seventy-three promised in June and the fifty promised in July were insufficient. He was taking gunners, ground personnel, navigators, and bombardiers from the mediums to increase his crews in the heavies and he urged Arnold to get crews from any source and rush him a minimum of 150 in June and 200 in July. In conclusion he summed up the crisis in trenchant phrases: "This battle against the German fighters is reaching its critical stage. We must press it at maximum. Any weakening or discouragement would be fatal. Repeat our greatest need more replacement crews, next more depot facilities, third get long range tanks for fighters. All must come through fast if we are to win this air battle this summer."

In his reply Arnold indicated some of the difficulties involved in keeping up a sufficient flow of crews to the theater. One aspect of the problem was the conflicting demand for precious resources. To continue this movement of replacements from the United States and to at the same time to maintain and increase the regular theater strength it would be necessary to shift planes from combat purposes to training, and that would hold down the number that could be sent to the theater. Furthermore, if the planned flow of replacements should be kept up—that is, two and one-half crews per plane in all heavy and medium groups, and two crews for all other types of aircraft in combat organizations— it would be impossible to turn out the additional combat crews needed for the scheduled build-up of strength in the United Kingdom between August 1943 and January 1944. "We are accordingly facing," he cabled, "one of the most serious decisions that we have had to make."

Replying two days later, Eaker definitely favored keeping up replacements even at the expense of new units, if necessary. He believed that ten groups maintained at full strength could exert much more pressure on the enemy than twenty groups at half strength with battle casualties not promptly replaced:

```
"I know now that we must keep our combat units up to organizational plan
and combat crew strength if we are to win the American bomber versus the
German fighter battle now in progress …hence we must get a higher flow
of replacement crews even at a sacrifice of some new units on schedule."
```

General Devers strongly concurred in these recommendations.

It is not clear from the available documents whether General Eaker's suggestions were accepted at this time. Certainly, the replacement crew crisis remained acute for the next two months. In July, 159 crews were received, but 171 were expended. In August 164 arrived and 120 were lost in operations, but in September there was a considerable improvement with 281 coming in and losses of 104. However, the heavy casualties in the early October operations made the situation critical again. On the 13th, just one day before the loss of 60 bombers and 60 crews (some 600 men) in the

Schweinfurt mission, Eaker was forced to cable that only 37 heavy crews had been received so far that month and replacements for the month were far below predictions. Following the Schweinfurt mission, he again cabled Arnold that replacements and crews must be rushed at once; he expected to lose 200 that month and need a minimum of 250. (That was a fairly close guess for actual losses came to 186.) In his reply General Arnold assured him that enough heavy bombers and crews were scheduled for delivery to insure his getting his minimum of 250. By the end of November incoming crews had brought the total (including casuals) for the United Kingdom up to 1,543 heavy-bomber crews and 1,187 fighter personnel.

Although, according to General Eaker, the shortage of combat crews was more of a factor in restricting operations than a shortage of planes, General Arnold was concerned over the large number of bombers reported as not ready for combat. It is perhaps significant that the previous week, General Spaatz had written him expressing his regret that the full weight of American bomber production had not been thrown against Germany proper. "I still believe that such an attack, if it had been followed through, may well have been decisive," Spaatz had written. On 2 June, Arnold cabled Eaker that "according to statistical reports too large percentage of your heavy bomber aircraft are reported not ready for combat ...I am much concerned over the limited number of aircraft reported ready for combat."

In the reply signed by General Devers, it was pointed out that two factors were keeping planes out of combat. The first was the need of making additional modifications on aircraft after their arrival in the theater because of special local needs. The second factor was battle damage. The strength of the enemy opposition was greater in this theater than in any other, and the battle damage caused by the GAF resistance was greater than had ever been contemplated. As yet, the repair organizations had not reached the necessary efficiency. As an example Devers cited a recent mission of twenty-eight planes of which all but one had received some battle damage. Of the 541 heavy bombers allocated to units, only 355, or 65.5 percent, were ready for combat.

This problem continued to disturb both the theater authorities and General Arnold throughout 1943. On 25 September, he was again urging General Eaker to keep only the minimum number of bombers in reserve or on the ground at bases; similar remarks can be found throughout the October and November cables and letters. Of course, the modification and maintenance situation partly caused the slow build-up of combat forces. Another factor was the fact that the bombers were not arriving from America in the numbers which the CBO planners had anticipated. This was especially disturbing to the British. On 15 August, the Chief of Air Staff, Sir Charles Portal, complained that the Eighth Air Force was considerable below the build-up as organized in POINTBLANK and approved at the Trident Conference. He urged that "the US Chiefs of Staff take all practicable steps to increase striking power of the VIII Bomber Command during the next two months." When General Arnold visited the theater and was able to see the situation for himself, he cabled General Marshall that it was necessary to send 200 B-17's to the theater at the earliest practical moment. Since twenty days were necessary to make the theater modifications, it would take until October at the earliest to get them all into combat. "The battle losses, battle damage and operational losses to the heavy bombers have cut down the number available to the organized groups so that they can not even approximate a total of thirty-five planes per group ready for service."

Even more critical was the fighter situation. On 1 July, when the total fighter strength with units consisted of 216 B-47's, Maj. Gen. Barney Giles, deputy commander of the Army Air Forces, sent a memo to his boss, General Arnold, stating that the Eighth Air Force lacked enough fighter forces to conduct escort operations. He recommended the ratio of one fighter group for each two heavy bombardment groups be established. Furthermore, he suggested the 20th Fighter Group, a P-38 organization destined for North Africa but still in America, be sent to England, and that three more P-38 groups both with the Twelfth also be transferred to the Eighth at the earliest opportunity. After some discussion, the question of the 20th Group was referred to the CCS, the Combined Chiefs of Staff, who agreed to send it to England. But nothing was done about the other three groups mentioned by General Giles, and so they remained in the Twelfth.

By August the fighter situation was somewhat improved by additional shipments airplanes that brought the number on hand with units up to 298. In September, the arrival of the first P-38's (all thirteen of them) plus additional Thunderbolts brought the total to 422. Since the twin-engine Lightening had a greater operational range than the Thunderbolt, General Arnold made special efforts to get P-38's into the Eighth Air Force as soon as possible. He finally decided to divert to Eaker all long-range type P-38's and P-51's promised to the Mediterranean and Pacific areas for the last quarter of 1943. This should provide Eaker with forty-five additional long-range P-38's in October, ninety-two in November and seventy-three in December above previous expectancies. Here again, the number sent to the theater remained considerably larger than the number that filtered through modification centers to become operational with combat units. The figures for the last four months of 1943 are as follows:

	P-38	P-47	P-51	Total with Units
September	13	409	0	422
October	74	480	1	555
November	68	587	21	676
December	53	741	44	838

Nevertheless, by the end of the year, the fighter strength had been greatly augmented and was no longer a pressing problem. The desire to increase the number of American fighters in the theater was closely connected with the growing menace of German fighter attacks on the bomber squadrons. It had been believed at one tine that the Fortress formations could fight their way through flak and enemy aircraft to the target and back without undue losses. The early missions in 1942 had tended to substantiate this theory, for losses were relatively light. However, by the spring of 1943, this comforting hypothesis was shot to pieces. General Spaatz had foreseen a time when the Germans would solve the problem of battling the B-17, and he warned this would be a severe setback. Unfortunately, it began to look as though his warning was coming true.

The first signs of trouble were noticed early in January 1943 when the GAF began to concentrate on frontal attacks, since it appeared that the firepower of the B-17 was weakest from this direction. General Eaker was forced to admit that "the Germans are making frontal attacks almost exclusively, and all our recent losses have resulted from this form of attack." However, he felt the front or chin turret would greatly reduce bomber casualties.

By April the Luftwaffe pilots had worked out new methods of assault that were hard to parry. In the Bremen raid of the 17th, which resulted in the loss of sixteen bombers, these new maneuvers seemed especially effective. Instead of striking indiscriminately at the formations, the Messerschmitt and Focke-Wulf fighters concentrated on the lead group as soon as they opened their bomb bay doors indicated the bombing run was begun, and that evasive action would be impossible. By this time, the Germans had a good idea of the limits of traverse of the nose guns, for pilots reported the heaviest attacks came from 10 o'clock and 2 o'clock, just outside the cone of fire and from just below the lower traverse limit of the guns. Other techniques tried, which would later become standard, included diving nose attacks from higher levels in which the plane acquired great speed; mass attacks by fighters in formation in line or abreast; and shelling of the formations with 40- or 50-mm. cannon by twin-engine fighters that paced the bombers just out of range. All of these methods proved to be effective, especially when the Germans learned to concentrate large masses of fighters at given points along the bomber routes.

By summer of 1943 the GAF had learned enough about the American heavy bombers and their tactics to put up a fierce defense when vital targets were threatened. The Eighth's attack on Kiel and Bremen on 13 June produced an unusually heavy air battle. It had been assumed that the 1st Wing, which was attacking Bremen, would bear the brunt of the enemy attack; consequently, it was made the stronger of the two. However, the formations were intercepted while still off the Danish coast, and the 4th Wing had to sustain violent assaults by some 200 enemy fighters. The 1st Wing losses were relatively light, but the 4th lost twenty-two aircraft. This habit of concentrating on one formation while leaving the other almost unmolested was a popular technique with the GAF. All types of attack and pursuit planes took part in the Kiel battle. The majority consisted of Me-109's and FW -190's, but Ju-88's, Me-110's, and Me-210's were also sighted. Attacks came from all angles with frontal assaults predominating; the fighters came in pairs, in 3's, 6's and 8's. Several attacks by six to eight planes abreast and in V's against the rear of the bomber formations were reported. Aerial bombing by enemy fighters was tried; the fighters dropped their bombs on the bombers, then attacked as soon as the bursts had dissipated with the apparent hope of upsetting the formation.

On the way home, as the bombers were just leaving the Dutch coast behind, there was another violent attack that lasted until the planes were within thirty-three miles of the English coast; a particular effort was made to pick off straggling Fortresses that could not keep up with the formations. Altogether, seventy-one percent of the returning planes were rendered temporarily inoperative from battle damage.

Ninety bombers were lost during June. While not a large number, perhaps, it represented eight percent of the attacking forces—this was considered serious. The percentage was only slightly lower in July, and at the beginning of August, General Arnold wrote General Eaker that he had asked the School of Applied Tactics to look into the matter very carefully and prepare a report on the best type of bombardment formation to be used over Germany. Furthermore, he had Hal Roach and other expert cameramen take photographs of various heavy-bomber formations employing nose and belly turrets so as to determine the best defense against enemy attack, especially those coming from the front.

#

Meanwhile, the air war went on. By now the GAF seldom rose in force to defend airdromes or similar installations in France, Belgium, or Holland, but deep penetrations of the Reich always produced a fight. Such was the result of the RAF attack on Schweinfurt and Regensburg on 17 August. These targets were extremely important to the production of German aircraft; therefore, they were defended "with determination, persistence and savageness seldom experienced by our crews before this mission." Entire squadrons made several attacks in line astern formations; packs of FW-190s and Me-109s came roaring down on the formations, spraying them with bullets on the approach, then passing through the groups to attack again. An interesting variation on the usual German methods was the vertical attack by diving enemy fighters to knock out the top turret; the attackers would then pass through the formations and seek a position for another strike.

The German controller handled his fighters well on this mission. It had been hoped that as the extent of British and American operations spread over more and more of northwest Europe, the German defense network would be badly strained. Unfortunately, such was not the case in 1943. The development of the air situation had evidently been foreseen and prepared for, and fighter pilots called out of their normal zone showed complete familiarity with the new combat area. At the same time, the controllers in France and Holland appeared to have a bird's-eye view of the raiders' progress into Germany; they knew in advance how to fit their units into the interception plans. In this case, the defense staffeln based in Holland pursued the Regensburg formations down the Rhine while their places were taken by other units transferred to the Holland area from northwest Germany. As a result, when the Schweinfurt raiders were returning to England, they were attacked over the Dutch area by these relatively fresh replacements, staffeln or fighters staggered from one base down to another to assure fresh crews were available.

One new development was reported which was destined to provide one of the severest tests of the Eighth Air Force. It can best be described by quoting from the Tactical Mission Report of this operation:

"Shortly after entering the enemy coast in, a pack of 7 FW-190s attacked the low squadron of our formation from the tail. They approached firing steadily with 20mm cannon and small caliber tracer ammunition. When these A/C were about 750 yards from our A/C, a very large flash burst from the center of each enemy aircraft (E/A), obliterating it from view. These E/A then dived under our formation. A second or two after the flash, several large black bursts appeared amongst our formation about one and one-half times as large as the ordinary flak burst. The projectile fired from theseE/A, and which was accompanied by the flash, could be followed with the unaided eye and appeared to be about three inches in diameter. This projectile burst in the air and not upon impact indicating a timed, rather than a percussion fuse. This attack crippled two of our A/C, who were forced out of formation and later brought down by a single attack."

Undoubtedly, this is a description of a rocket attack which, though not the first instance, was certainly one of the best observed. Actually, the use of rockets against Fortress formations had been suspected as early as 29 April, although British Air Ministry Intelligence did not take much stock in the early rumors of such a weapon. On 1 June, a report was submitted containing a brief description of the German rocket gun. It pointed out that equipped with such a weapon, "one group of German planes could easily raise hell with a fortress formation if no countermeasures were taken."

After the Schweinfurt and Regensburg missions, there was little doubt that the GAF had perfected a new aerial weapon whose development and use has already been foreseen by Alexander de Jeversky in his Victory Through Air Power. In a memo for the Commanding General of the Army Air Forces, Col. A. W. Brock, Jr. assistant Chief of Air Staff, Intelligence, recommended that we should expend every effort to work out a defense up to 2,500 yards for our heavy bomber formations; General Giles advised General Eaker that the situation was being studied in Washington. As tentative solutions to the problem, he suggested that Eaker consider increasing his fighter support so as to provide successive waves of escorts; or perhaps employ specially trained bomber formation leaders with extra armor on the planes. Arnold cabled his response from the theater that the situation was serious. The rocket development of the GAF had reached a point where it was hazardous to our heavy operations, and there was evidence that planes had been hit by rockets, thereby causing great damage. These rockets were usually lobbed into the formations from distances of 100 to 1,700 yards. He urged that counter-measures be initiated immediately to protect the bombers.

Meanwhile, the Germans had perfected their tactics for using rocket-firing planes in combination with single-engine fighters; as a result, they were able to stage one of the most costly battles of the air war when the Eighth attacked Schweinfurt on 14 October. In the words of General Eaker, "It was the final countermeasure to our daylight bombing ...a full scale dress rehearsal perfectly timed and executed." Concentrating on one bomber wave, a force of single-engine fighters attacked very close from the front firing 20-mm. cannon and machine guns. As they broke away, they were followed by large numbers of twin-engine aircraft with rockets fastened under the wings. The rockets were lobbed in barrage quantities into the bomber formations with the firing beginning at long-range. While this maneuver was being carried out, the fighters were refueling and upon taking the air again, they at once attacked from all directions, while the twin-engine planes re-formed and prepared to deliver new rocket assaults. The Germans skillfully massed all their forces against one formation and after the rockets were expended, the fighters concentrated on eliminating the crippled bombers. In this way, one combat wing was practically wiped out, losing twenty-nine planes out of forty-nine attacking. The total losses were 60 bombers out of an effective force of 226.

This casualties caused something of a stir. The War Department was especially concerned over the successful employment of rockets by the Germans. General Marshall cabled Eaker that he was "intensely interested in your message describing the German rocket technique in their attack on your formations and I feel certain that you and your people will find quickly a means of reducing this hazard." General Arnold cabled that "we must be equally versatile in our technique and original in our ideas if we are going to continue these operations with any degree of success." He then inquired as to the countermeasures General Eaker proposed to take.

In response, the general indicated a considerable change in the scope of his operations. He intended to try multiple attacks by seven or eight combat wings of fifty-four bombers each on widely dispersed targets; this, he hoped, would force a thinning out of enemy defenses. He also said he wanted to use more fighter cover at longer range and urged Arnold to send him every available plane of this type. Greater emphasis was to be placed on counter air force operations by attacking the fields with the bombers recently transferred to the Ninth Air Force, and by pressing the destruction of factories and repair establishments with the heavy bombers. Eaker concluded with a request for more bombers and crews, more fighters and more long-range fuel tanks.

By this time it was clear that our margin of success in the air war was a narrow one at best, and a means to provide additional protection for the bomber formations had to be discovered. Certainly, the Eighth could not afford any missions, which resulted in the loss of 60 planes and battle damage to 145. The English had been skeptical of the whole idea of daylight attacks, and one American general had already suggested that pending the acquisition of bases on the Continent itself, the Eighth should give up its daylight raids and confine itself to night attacks. If the American bombardment doctrine was to avoid a complete revision, something would have to be done to counter German fighter and rocket attacks on the heavy bombers.

A solution to this problem been sought for some time. General Spaatz proposed one of the first ideas. Writing General Arnold on 29 April 1942, he suggested auxiliary fuel tanks seemed to offer the only immediate solution to extending the range of fighters, "unless it can be developed that the bomber, with its firepower, can substitute ammunition for bomb load and act as an accompanying fighter." Whether or not General Spaatz's suggestion led to any action at that time is not clear. However, about the beginning of 1943, it was decided to convert a certain number of Fortresses for escort work. These planes, known as YB-40, would carry no bombs, but were to be provided with chin turrets to increase the forward power and with additional belly and top guns. Armor was to be distributed liberally; all essential engine and fuel accessories were to be well covered with steel sheeting up to one half inch in thickness, and sections of the fuselage were protected. Good results were expected from this experiment, as there was considerable pressure from theater commanders to get the YB-40 into combat. Ten deliveries to the Eighth Air Force had been several times postponed, as General Eaker protested vigorously that he needed them badly and wanted them hurried up. Eventually, the planes reached him and on 22 June 1943, a force of 11 YB-40s accompanied 297 bombers on a mission to industrial targets near Antwerp.

Unfortunately, it was not a success. After several operations, General Eaker was regretfully forced to write General Giles that "our tactical people insist that they do not want this aeroplane." The objections seem to have been due to the greatly increased weight of the ship. Owing to its extra guns and armor, it became so heavy that it could not climb as fast as the regular B-17 formations. As a result, when the YB-40's accompanied bombers, they upset the formations. Then it was decided to try them out as "wingmen", and two of them were used to fly protection for the leaders of each combat wing. Here again, their quite different flying characteristics caused trouble, rendering them useless. By the 11th of October, it was decided to use them in flexible gunnery schools in the United States as they could not be used in the theater.

At least one good thing came from the YB-40 experiment. The value of the chin turret as a means of strengthening the forward fire power was made evident, and this later became standard equipment. Additional improvements on the Flying Fortress included better sights for all turrets, reflector gun sights for flexible, hand-held guns, and better frontal armor. Likewise, the B-24 received additional forward guns and an improved turret for the tail position.

Another attempt to meet the GAF attack led to the development of blind-bombing techniques. That bombing could be carried out when the overcast made it difficult for the enemy fighters to assemble; at the same time, bad weather over the target would no longer keep the bombing planes bound to their bases. British developed the first successful blind-bombing techniques and equipment, which were used by the Eighth Air Force. By the latter part of July 1943, the War Department had approved a tasking order for a pathfinder (blind-bombing) force, and the first squadron was soon training at the radar laboratories at the Massachusetts Institute of Technology. At the same time, a prototype B-17 was being fitted up for this sort of work at the Aircraft Radio Laboratory, Wright Field, and early in September the first pathfinder units moved to England.

By the end of September four planes were equipped with a British H2S radar bombing device, and it was decided not to wait for additional equipment. These four planes were used to lead 338 bombers to Eaden on 27 September. The combat wing led by the H2S planes was to bomb on the leader and the following units were to bomb on sky markers left by the pathfinder planes. Unfortunately, the clouds went up to 20,000 feet and the markers were not visible. Nevertheless, General Anderson commanding the VIII Bomber Command and his combat leaders considered the experiment encouraging. As a result, General Eaker cabled General Arnold that every effort should be made to get an H2X squadron to England by 15 November, and to provide 30 percent monthly replacements. (H2X was the American version of the British H2S bombing radar.) He believed that overcast bombing might be the answer to the German fighter and was anxious to improve the technique. By the end of October the Eighth was using additional blind-bombing devices; by the end of November, pathfinder missions were a regular feature of operations.

But none of these developments really met the threat of the German fighter attack on the bomber formations. The real answer was to provide more Mustangs and Thunderbolts for the "big friends" on their deep penetrations. General Doolittle had stressed this point in a memo to the head of Army Air Forces on 22 May 1943. He pointed out that in the Northwest African Air Forces, there was a serious shortage of long-range fighter escorts. If escort fighters could be used, losses would be reduced, the bombing would be improved, and the psychological effects would be so favorable that crews could be sent more frequently on missions. Furthermore, the new German methods of air-to-air bombing, heavy attacks by strongly armored fighters, and long-range machine-gun attacks could only be met by more fighters. "Although escort fighters have been desirable in the past," the General concluded prophetically, "they will be essential in the future."

Granted that long-range fighters were necessary, how was the range of the P-38, P-51, and the P-47 to be extended until they could provide fighter protection all the way out and back for the bombers? The answer had been given by General Spaatz in 1942 when he wrote: "Auxiliary (expendable) tanks offer the only immediate solution for extending the range of fighters."

On 3 October 1942 the question was raised by the theater authorities as to the possibility of the United States furnishing jettisonable belly tanks for fighters. The first P-38's in the theater had possessed two 150-gallon tanks as standard equipment, but shortly after reaching England, the P-38's were transferred to North Africa. Nothing was done about the tanks during the remainder of 1942, but in early 1943 the question was taken up again. The Air Technical Section of the VIII Fighter Command was investigating the possibility of having the tanks made in England, but it was first decided to obtain the equipment from the United States if possible; on 18 February, a request was sent out for 60,000. Owing to the immediate need for them, Washington decided to request the British Ministry of Aircraft Production (MAP) to supply 46,000 jettisonable tanks of 200 gallon capacity for the P-47 aircraft. The MAP instead countered with the suggestion that the tanks be made in the United States, then shipped for assembly to England. This plan was rejected. Meanwhile, the Air Technical Service worked out a design for a steel tank which was approved by the Eighth Air Force on 29 May and the British were requested to manufacture it in quantity. Owing to the current steel shortage in the British Isles the MAP offered instead to construct 108-gallon paper tanks of British design reinforced to withstand

seven pounds per inch working pressure. The VIII Fighter Command
approved this paper tank on 26 June, with the initial delivery made on 12
July. A short time later the first mission was flown with the paper tanks—
and was successful.

But the paper tanks were not the final solution, and since 4,000 metal
tanks of 75-gallon capacity had recently arrived from the United States, it
was decided to try equipping the P-47 (which had the shortest range of the
three principal fighter types) with them, pending the availability of the
larger paper tanks. It was believed that the Thunderbolt should be able to
climb to 22,000 feet and travel 140 to 150 miles before having to drop the
tank. The first flight tests of the P-47 with the metal tank were run off on 17
August and were successful. One week later the P-47's were sent on a
combat mission with this equipment.

Meanwhile, the 108-gallon paper tank had reached production; on 3
September, the British made their first delivery to the Eighth Air Force.
However, as the steel situation in the United Kingdom eased somewhat, it
was decided to manufacture steel tanks of 100 and 150 gallons. When the
P-51 arrived in the theater, it complicated the situation since it had equipment for two 75-gallon external tanks. But because they were unpressurized
and could not be used at altitudes of over 20,000 feet, they were not desirable. It was finally decided to transfer the P-47 tanks to the P-51 as needed,
and a temporary installation for the 108-gallon paper tank was worked out
for the Thunderbolt.

Thus the difficulties were eliminated little by little. At the end of September there were enough fighters equipped with jettisonable fuel con-
tainers to go on a long-range escort mission. On the 27th, the day that saw
the first pathfinder operation, the bombers that went to Emden were
escorted to the target and back by long-range P-47 fighters. By November
enough planes were being equipped with the smaller tanks so that the radius
of penetration and, withdrawal support had greatly increased. By 14
December the shipments of British tanks were so large that production of
the 75-gallon container was stopped in the United States and at the end of
the year there were between 2,000 and 3,000 jettisonable tanks at each VIII
Fighter Command station. In 1944 the fighters would be able to accompany the bombers virtually to any target.

The long-range American fighter plane was the answer to the rocket and fighter combined attack on the heavy bombers. At the end of October, General Arnold could still write: "My concern about the fighter opposition that the Eighth Air Force bombers are meeting is very great." But after October the bomber losses never seriously threatened the build-up of strength in the United Kingdom. By May, only 2.7 percent of the bombers reaching the target were destroyed. In this victory, the adaptation of the single-engine fighter to long-range work played a large part. In the opinion of Wing Commander Nigel Tangye, it was "one of the most remarkable achievements of the war." Nor was the significance of this lost on the Germans. During his interrogation, Herman Goering, stated he could hardly believe it when told that American fighters had appeared over Hanover, and he realized it was a tragic development for Germany.

Thus, as the winter of 1943-44 approached, some of the problems of the Eighth Air Force seemed to have been resolved. The increasing flow of planes and crews from the United States relieved fears that the offensive against Germany might fail for lack of strength and material. It seemed unlikely that diversions to other projects would threaten POINTBLANK, and the appearance of the long-range fighter made it probable that by the first of the year, the bomber squadrons would have complete fighter protection to the target and back.

Nevertheless, General Arnold was not satisfied with the progress of POINTBLANK. The production of German fighters had been held down to approximately 400 Me-109's and 200 FW-190's per month for the last quarter of 1943, but the Luftwaffe was far from destroyed. With the restriction of bombing operations which the winter weather would undoubtedly cause, it might be able to increase its production. On the day of the great Schweinfurt mission, Arnold communicated some of his dissatisfaction to Air Marshal Sir Charles Portal. "OVERLORD hangs directly on the success of our combined aerial offensive," he began, "and I am sure that our failure to decisively cripple both the sources of German air power and the GAF itself is causing you and me real concern." General Arnold then stated he felt not enough planes were getting off the ground, and that he was "pressing" Eaker on this.

He was likewise disturbed over deviations from the CBO priorities to such targets as shipbuilding installations, port cities, and the like, and he was also anxious to see more British fighters go into action. Two days later he cabled Portal that the great effort being expended against the German aircraft industry by our heavy bombers would not show any early results unless the present front-line strength of the GAF could be severely crippled. "We must bring into the battle against him all of our numerical superiority in aircraft. By this I mean specifically the aircraft of our tactical forces, your home defense forces, and the total weight of our combined bomber forces against the installations mutually selected for destruction."

In his reply on the 24th of October, Air Marshal Portal disagreed with certain parts of General Arnold's letter of the 14th while he agreed with others. He stated definitely that none of the official priorities had been altered in any way. The attacks to which Arnold had objected were dictated by reason of the training needs of crews, and because of the low number of crews and aircraft which did not permit of deep or frequent penetration into heavily defended areas. General Eaker had been asked to attack targets outside of Germany proper only when weather prevented operations against more important objectives.

As to the failure to destroy the Luftwaffe, the main difficulty was to force the German to come up and fight. "I fear that this is not always successful since his policy is to conserve his fighters and to use them only against large bomber formations which penetrate deep into the heart of his country."

On the other hand, the air marshal admitted that in the CBO, they had "fallen far short of what we hoped to accomplish." For one thing, the RAF bombers had to concentrate on Ruhr targets due to the short summer nights. Also, it was difficult at night to locate the small towns in which many of the aircraft factories were located. The Eighth Air Force had been held back due to its slow build-up. It had by now come within seventy percent of what had been anticipated for October, but its effective strength was only fifty percent of what had been expected as available for Phase I of the CBO. Thus, a great tactical advantage had been thrown away by the delay in the accumulation of strength, and the enemy had been able to handle this small force while developing adequate countermeasures. Portal now believed that, unless it was decided to accept heavy casualties, it would take a greater force than that provided for in the CBO to achieve the anticipated effect.

It is evident that both Arnold and Portal felt a critical period lay ahead. Given an unusually bad winter with many nonoperational days and overcast targets, the GAF might succeed in recovering from the losses it sustained in the heavy attacks of July, August and October. Much would depend on the operations of the next four months. New bases for the attack on the Luftwaffe and a few good days of flying weather in the winter might decide the success of the land invasion of the Continent in 1944.

4

THE WINTER OFFENSIVE AGAINST THE GAF - NOVEMBER 1943 TO FEBRUARY 1944

With the November operations, a fundamental change took place in the conduct of the offensive against the Luftwaffe and German aircraft production: the Eighth Air Force ceased to be the sole executant of the plan. The activation of the Ninth Air Force in the European Theater of Operations (ETO) on 16 October and the Fifteenth Air Force on 1 November brought new forces into the air war, and new bases from which hitherto unscathed targets might be attacked.

The Ninth developed out of a need to expand the VIII Air Support Command. In preparation for the counter invasion, it was arranged to increase the fighters and medium bombers of the VIII Air Support Command until it became virtually a tactical air force operation under the Eighth. However, when it was decided to combine both American and RAF tactical aircraft under the overall supervision of Air Marshal Sir Trafford Leigh-Mallory, it seemed best to create a new American air force for this purpose, although the operational control of the Eighth would take control of the organization for combat missions. The new commander of this force was Lt. Gen. Lewis Brereton, formerly commander of the Ninth Air Force in the Middle East.

In deference to his wishes, the new name of his old command was transferred to his new post. On 18 October, the new Ninth Air Force came into being in England and would function as a tactical air force supporting the Eight.

#

The establishment of a new strategic air force in the Mediterranean theater was a much more complicated and involved matter. The main purpose of operations in this area had been to (1) destroy the Axis forces in North Africa, (2) eliminate Italy from the air, and (3) secure bases in Italy for operations against Germany. The air organizations involved in these campaigns were the Ninth (later losing its heavy bombers to the Twelfth and giving its name, commanding general, and headquarters to the tactical air force in the United Kingdom), and the Northwest African Strategic Air Force, a mixed heavy and medium bomber outfit under the command of General Spaatz since 26 February 1943. Spaatz had witnessed the desirable effects of aerial blows against German industry and air installations. In an exchange of letters in the summer of 1945 between Spaatz and General Hap Arnold, it seems the two air strategists were thinking in terms of major air operations from Italian air bases. On the 27th of June, Spaatz wrote Arnold as follows:

```
"I have been very much concerned as to what will happen to the Air Forces
here after the next operation or two. It seems very desirable that the
heavy bomber effort against Germany be applied from more than one base area.
If we can establish ourselves in Italy, much of Germany can be reached from
the air with better weather conditions at our airdromes then prevail
normally in England. This would immediately, when applied, force a
dispersion of German fighter and anti-aircraft defenses."
```

In his reply on the 28th, General Arnold stated that his idea of a number one priority was a heavy attack on the German fighter establishments. On 14 August, he again emphasized to Spaatz the effect of a sustained strategic bombardment on German key industrial targets from Mediterranean bases would justify giving this type of operation a top priority.

Support for a strategic bombing offensive from Italian bases also came from General Eisenhower. After the crisis at the Salerno beachhead had abated (where Salerno refers to the invasion of mainland Italy and the landing of Allied forces), and it looked as if a fairly rapid advance might take place, he wrote General Marshal that he and General Spaatz believed a greater effectiveness might be achieved with less loss if a portion of the bomber offensive could be applied from Italy during the winter months. This would make it possible to attack targets beyond reach of Britain-based bombers, there would be less GAF and anti-aircraft opposition generally, and the Luftwaffe would have to thin itself out to meet attacks from two directions. Said Eisenhower: "Since one of the major reasons for the move into Italy was to secure air bases for this type of operation, I feel that it is a matter which should receive early consideration."

On 20 August, General Arnold prepared a memo entitled "Command and Control of Strategic Air Forces Operating Against Germany." Although primarily concerned with the question of command, this document went into the desirability of establishing a new strategic air force in Italy. Arnold felt that with suitable airfields in this peninsula, the carrying out of air actions against German industry would be facilitated by the alternative use of British and Italian bases depending on the weather. Since he believed the weather in the Po Valley would probably be better for bombers than that in England, it would be useful to have some airdromes in this area. Shuttle operations between England and Italy could also be carried out.

At this point, opposition to the plan developed. The British air authorities were strongly opposed to diverting heavy groups to Italy, and certain American generals in the ETO were dubious about the idea. On 29 September Air Marshal Sir Arthur Harris wrote General Eaker that he was seriously disturbed by the belief that bombers operating from Italy could do more damage to Germany than planes coming from English bases. He thought many important production centers were closer to Britain and weather conditions in the plains of Italy were no better than England's. Furthermore, since the Italy-based planes would have to make a detour to preserve the neutrality of Switzerland, this would add to their journey besides simplifying the German fighter defense. In conclusion he stated:

"It would take at least a year before a ponderable force of heavy bombers could be operated economically from Northern Italy—after we have taken Northern Italy. For these reasons, I am convinced the advantages to be gained from using bases in Italy are negligible. The loss of striking power

against the vital parts of Germany, and of time, which would be incurred by
transferring bombers to them from this country would, on the other hand, be
quite disastrous."

General Eaker was opposed to the plan as well because he feared it would cut into his bomber and fighter forces and make difficult the accomplishment of POINTBLANK. Maj. Gen. Idwal H. Edwards, Chief of Staff for US Operations in Europe, wondered if sufficient consideration had been given to the idea. Like the British, he questioned the value and availability of Italian bases and felt that already existing facilities in the United Kingdom were adequate. He was afraid shuttle operations would require more service personnel in both areas; if the Bradley Plan, the troop build-up for the Eighth Air Force, was not met in the United Kingdom, how would this larger demand be satisfied? Air Marshal Norman H. Bottomley warned that "we must avoid precipitate action which may result in sending aircraft and resources to the Mediterranean only to find them unable to contribute effectively from that theater."

At this point, the opposing arguments can be summarized briefly. General Arnold advocated the creation of a new strategic air force operating from Italian bases for the following reasons: (1) it would enable our bombers to reach objectives out of range of Britain-based planes; (2) it would divide German fighter strength; (3) it would make possible shuttle bombing between England and Italy; and (4) weather conditions in northern Italy would make possible winter operations against the Reich when British bases would be frequently nonoperational.

These arguments were apparently opposed by Harris, Portal, Bottomley, Eaker, and Edwards on the following grounds: (1) the most important German targets could already be reached from the United Kingdom; (2) Italian weather was quite as foul as the British variety; (3) to avoid Switzerland would greatly add to the length and danger of each mission; and (4) to set up a new strategic air force would seriously weaken the operations of the Eighth. (Perhaps the British and Americans in England were thinking of what happened to the Eighth's operations and supply system when the Twelfth was set up in the Mediterranean area.)

In view of the later operations of the Fifteenth Air Force, which in fact would be created after the debates were concluded, it is possible to make some sort of an estimate of these arguments. British claims that most of the important German targets were within reach of RAF, and Eighth Air Force bombers seem to have failed to take into account the eastward dispersion of the aircraft industry. An Office of Strategic Services report of 17 August 1943 estimated that only 12 percent of the German single-engine fighter assembly was carried out within 500 miles of London, while slightly over 80 percent was located within about 400 miles of possible north Italian bases. Actually, in addition to the bombing of the great complex of Wiener Neu-stadt, attacks on important Italian, Hungarian, and Yugoslav aircraft facto-ries would have been impossible without the Fifteenth. Furthermore, the easterly dispersal of the GAF plants completely knocked out the argument based on preserving the neutrality of Switzerland. The bomber routes lay far to the east of that nation.

On the other hand there is no question but that the English were right about the weather. Climatic conditions, according to Maj.Gen. Nathan F. Twining, commander of the Fifteenth after 3 January 1944, greatly hin-dered the Fifteenth's pursuit of POINTBLANK during January and Feb-ruary, and weather effectually prevented shuttle bombing and many com-bined operations.

It is difficult to say how much the German fighters were split by the attack from Italy. Had it been possible to run more combined operations, there might be more evidence upon which to make a judgment; but as pointed out above, the weather usually interfered.

It is also next to impossible to estimate how much greater the Eighth's operations would have been without the establishment of the Fifteenth. Since the principal obstacle to carrying out the air offensive against the Luft-waffe was weather rather than a lack of planes, perhaps the question is aca-demic.

In spite of opposing arguments, General Arnold prepared a "Plan to Assure the Most Effective Exploitation of the Combined Bomber Offen-sive" and submitted it to the Joint Chiefs of Staff about 9 October. This pro-vided for the establishment of a strategic air force in Italy to be formed by combing the six heavy groups of the XII Bomber Command with thirteen groups to be diverted from allocations to the Eighth. The scheduled build-up was to bring the Fifteenth up to twenty-one heavy bombardment groups, one reconnaissance, and seven long-range fighter groups by the end of April 1944. After being approved by JCS, it reached the CCS and received their approval on 22 October, with activation of the Fifteenth scheduled for the beginning of November. Even after this decision, there was still some discussion. At the CCS meeting on 29 October, Sir John Dill voiced his doubts as to the wisdom of creating a new diversion from the bomber effort. As far as additional groups went, he was sure the facilities in England were fully prepared to take them. General Arnold replied that General Spaatz would be able to accommodate them in Italy; General Marshall said he was concerned over the losses of the Eighth Air Force and felt it was essential to create a new air or bomber force to help disperse the German fighters. Apparently this ended the discussion; on 1 November, the Fifteenth was formally activated under Maj. Gen. James Doolittle with 283 bombers and 262 fighters on hand with units.

#

Immediately after the establishment of the new strategic force, the question of its control was settled. In a directive of 23 October, it was ordered that the theater commander, General Eisenhower, they see to it that the operations of the Fifteenth were to be closely coordinated with the Eighth to improve the effectiveness of their operations against targets of the combined bomber offensive. At the same time, in case of a strategic or tactical exigencies, he was authorized to use the Fifteenth for purposes "other than its primary mission," informing the CSS of the action taken. Once the Fifteenth was established, General Arnold made it very clear that barring the expectations noted, he did not intend it to be diverted from it objectives.

There were four objectives of the new air force: (1) to destroy the German Air Force; (2) to participate in the land battle in Italy; (3) to continue POINTBLANK operations; and (4) to weaken the German position in the Balkans. Operations against the aircraft and air installations were to be carried out whenever a profitable return offered itself. Special attention was would be paid to German-held airdromes in southern France and to a list of seven German aircraft manufacturing plants.

#

On 8 November, an important meeting was held in Gibraltar to coordinate final arrangements in which Generals Eaker and Doolittle and Air Marshall Tedder took part. An understanding was reached as to the proper allocation of targets between the two strategic air forces, and procedures were set up to facilitate the many combined operations expected to take place involving the Eighth and Fifteenth. To ensure the rapid exchange of operational experiences and intelligence gathered, liaison officers were to be exchanged between the two headquarters. As a result of this meeting, a complete agreement was reached on problems common to both strategic organizations.

Meanwhile, the Fifteenth had already become operational on 2 November by one of the great raids of the war against the Messerschmitt factory at Wiener Neustadt. It will be recalled that this complex had been attacked in August by the old Ninth Air Force, with considerable damage done. It was believed that the Germans planned to double the factory's output by 1944, but the August attack had delayed these plans. By the end of October some of the damage had been repaired, and work was just starting on a large building in Werke II, which was supposed to be making Me-109 fuselages and was a known important unit in the expansion plans. Consequently, the raid of 2 November was well timed.

A great deal of careful preparation was involved in this mission. The distance that the bombers had to fly from their Sicilian bases was more than 1,000 miles round-trip; 600 of those miles were over enemy-held territory. Since this made it possible for the GAF to make many interceptions, the fighter escort was to be extended to the maximum range, which would give the bombers protection within 100 miles of the target. Another group of fighters would then meet the formations at maximum range and escort them back to their bases.

Shortly after noon on the 2d, most of the operational aircraft of the Fifteenth took off, heading northward. Apparently intimidated by the attendant fighter groups, enemy interceptors based on the nearby fields did not take the air, and no serious fighter opposition appeared until about ten minutes before the target was reached. A total of 112 Liberators and Fortresses dropped 327 tons of high explosive in spite of attacks by 150 to 175 enemy planes. The results were most gratifying: one aircraft assembly plant was destroyed and another damaged; two flight hangars were wiped out; and many buildings showed blast damage. Bomb craters spotted the Wiener Neustadt/Lord airfield and thirteen aircraft were damaged on the ground. Buildings in the southwest corner of the plant and the adjoining labor camp were hit, with some machine shops in the factory struck. Eleven bombers were lost and claims of 56-27-8 were filed. It was believed that this raid deprived the Luftwaffe of a monthly output of approximately 250 of their best fighters, or 40 percent of the total output of the Me-109.

While the Fifteenth was making this impressive debut, the Eighth was progressing rapidly in its development of blind-bombing techniques. In the largest daylight operation yet carried out by American planes, on 11 November a total of 1,233 bombers and fighters attacked German targets using H2X leader planes, although F2S equipment was present in case the H2X failed. The results were satisfactory, and General Arnold instructed the Fifteenth to send certain officers to the United States to help organize a Pathfinding unit for the new strategic air force. He contemplated sending eight B-24's equipped with H2X and crews in January and 16 more in February for the training.

Another big H2X mission took place on 13 November when 317 heavy bombers attacked Bremen, covered by 10/10 cloud. Evidently the Germans had learned the overcast was no longer adequate protection, for the mission was strongly contested, and a fierce air battle took place over the clouds.

On 8 November, the Fifteenth began a series of attacks against ball-bearing installations lasting three days. The Turin works were bombed on the first day; on the 9th and 10th, the Villar-Perosa aircraft machine gun plant slightly west of Turin was the target. The mission of the 8th was successful, and the mission intelligence summary estimated that the factory would be completely inoperative for some time to come. The missions against Villar-Perosa were not so effective; the first attack missed the target entirely, and the second caused only slight damage.

After five days of inactivity, the Fifteenth turned from ball bearings to airfields. The first target was, by request, the Athens/Eleusis airdrome. This was the most active long-range bomber field in Greece. Between sixty to seventy aircraft were usually based there, including a large number of Ju-88's which had been operating against islands in the Dodecanese group held by the allies. The island of Leros, where the Germans had seized a beachhead, was under especially heavy attack by enemy formations based at Eleusis. Consequently, it was hoped that a successful blow against it might ease the pressure at Leros. The field was bombed by 46 B-24's with fragmentation bombs during the morning of the 15th with some success. However, a much more successful raid occurred on the 17th when 40 B-17's dropped 120 tons of 500-pound GP bombs with a heavy concentration on hangars, buildings, and the landing area west of the central runway. There were probable direct hits on five of the nine hangars and a direct hit on the central administration building. Of the fifty-five aircraft seen on the field, ten were damaged and five were destroyed. On the 18th Athens/Eleusis was struck again by 50 B-17's dropping 6,900 fragmentation bombs to complete the destruction caused by the heavier explosives used the previous day. By this time the field was so thoroughly postholed as to be temporarily inoperative.

Meanwhile on the 16th, bombers of the Fifteenth Air Force carried out a raid on two airdromes in southern France, thus fulfilling one of the requirements of their bombing directive. Istres le Tube and Salon de Provence, both in France, were bombed by 85th and 43rd, the two medium bomb groups in the Fifteenth Air Force. The B-26 bombers ran off this mission with good results.

On the 18th the Eighth made one of its longest flights to bomb the GAF airplane engine and fuselage repair depot at the Oslo/Kjeller airdrome Norway. Owing to the distance involved, no fighters could accompany the dispatched 102 B-24's. A total of 78 Liberators reached the target and bombed from the relatively low altitude of 12,000 feet to insure accuracy with very good results . The C. L. Brinker Eisenwerke Airframe Repair Factory was severely damaged with hits on the dismantling shop, a storage depot, offices for production and blue prints, the heat treatment establishment, FW-190 and Me-109 component storage building, and other installations. The Daimler Benz Aero Engine Repair factory had two main buildings almost completely demolished, and the Bayerische Motorenwerke (BMW) Aero Engine Repair Factory was still burning when the photo reconnaissance was made. As the planes retired from the targets, fires were burning fiercely, there were heavy explosions, and a column of smoke arose that could be seen twenty-five miles away.

Operations of both air forces for the remainder of November were not especially outstanding. Weather constantly interfered; many missions had to be canceled and the results of those carried out often went unobserved. Some Wellingtons of the Fifteenth bombed the Turin ball-bearing works and Rome's Ciampino airdrome in night raids with undisclosed results. Somewhat better luck was had when medium bombers attacked the Grosseto airdrome in Italy with 93.5 tons of 500-pound GP bombs.

The Eighth concluded its November operations by two attacks on the town of Solingen in the Rhineland. This town was an aircraft parts and steel alloy center. In both missions the weather prevented an assessment of the damage. On the second mission on 1 December, the fighter escort stayed with the bombers until the Initial Point (IP) for the bomb run was reached where upon the "little friends" withdrew. The formations were then attacked viciously by GAF fighters and twenty-four bombers were lost.

November was not an important month for POINTBLANK operations. The most important operation was the Fifteenth's attack on Wiener Neustadt on the 2d; for the most part, however, both strategic Air Forces confined their efforts against the Luftwaffe to attacks on airdromes and repair installations. Claims were considerably less than in previous months. The Eighth listed a total of 222 enemy aircraft destroyed, and the Fifteenth credited its aircraft with 135 kills. The Eighth lost ninety-five planes, the Fifteenth twenty-eight. The newly organized Ninth Air Force confined itself almost entirely to bomber attacks on airdromes in northwest France, Belgium, and the important Amsterdam/Schiphol airport in Holland, while its fighters often escorted the heavy bombers of the Eighth over the Continent.

In December, the weather continued to restrict the operations of the Fifteenth Air Force, and the POINTBLANK program suffered especially. Airdromes were the principal target, with several attacks being made against GAF bases near Athens. The Fiat Ball Bearing Works at Turin, which had been twice raided in November, was visited again by 118 B-17's for the first mission of the month on 1 December. Coverage of the target by some 354 tons of bombs was regarded as complete by the returning bombers, and later reconnaissance reported considerable damage to the factory. Prior to these attacks, the Fiat plant was supposed to produce forty percent of all the ball bearings available to Germany; it was now believed that two months output had been eliminated.

The Rome/Casale airdrome was attacked without opposition on 3 December by a small force of Liberators dropping 32.24 tons of fragmentation and 16 tons of GP bombs. On the 6th, a series of raids on the Athenian airdromes began with attacks on the field installations at Athens/Eleusis and Athens/Kalamaki. The attack on Eleusis was made by 45 B-17's escorted by 33 P-38's. Fragmentation bombs were dropped with fair success, but the photo coverage was not good; an exact estimate seems to be lacking. The Kalamaki airdrome vas first bombed by 500-pound GP bombs, then hit by 4,250 fragmentation bombs. Dust and debris made it difficult to assess the damage. In both cases, these attacks provoked a certain GAF reaction, but the air battles were usually small affairs and not very costly to either side.

Another attack was made on the Greek fields on the 8th. Eleusis was raided again and well covered with 8,172 fragmentation bombs. The Athens/Tatoi field revealed a concentration of 42 aircraft, and so it was hit by 38 Liberators dropping 4,000 of the 20-pound antiaircraft and antipersonnel bombs. It was estimated that fourteen aircraft were destroyed on the ground, including seven bomber-transport types. Later reconnaissance confirmed this, and credited the attacking forces with wiping out twenty-one aircraft at the Eleusis airdrome. Again on the 14th, Liberators and Fortresses of the Fifteenth attacked the three Athenian fields with P-38 and P-47 escorts. Tatoi was well covered and seven hangars received direct hits or near misses; the runway and west dispersal area were a mass of smoke and debris as the bombers retired from the area. Kalamaki was hit by the largest task force (76 bombers) of the three, dropping 224.5 tons of 500-pound GP explosives. Between 15 and 20 FW-190's and Me-109's were encountered over the target, with 8 claimed as destroyed. During the attack, twenty-nine enemy planes were counted on the airfield of which eight were destroyed and seven believed damaged. There were heavy concentrations of hits on the hangar area, storage facilities, landing strips and runways, and dispersal areas.

A final blow was struck on the 20th when Eleusis was heavily bombed by a task force of 109 B-17's escorted by 66 P-38's. The defense was the stiffest yet encountered over the Greek airdromes. Both flak and planes were well controlled, and the tactics had obviously been planned in advance by experienced personnel. The bombing was considered successful; many buildings were struck and the field was well holed. Three bombers were lost.

The only attempt made to bomb a high-priority POINTBLANK target occurred on 19 December when a small force attempted to bomb a Messerschmitt factory at in southern Germany. Unfortunately, the strike photos contained nothing but an excellent view of the cloud cover over the target, and visual estimates indicated that the bombs fell south of the objective. Five Liberators were lost.

A final blow was struck at airfields when Medium bombers of the Fifteenth (the 17th and 319th groups) attacked Guidonia and Centecello on 28 December. Strike photos showed eighteen aircraft on the ground at Guidonia with seven destroyed and one damaged. The bomb pattern covered the field. At Centecello, bomb strikes were distributed over the southeast side of the field only.

POINTBLANK targets within range of the Eighth Air Force did not come in for much bombing during December. Weather conditions often made deep penetrations of the Continent impossible; consequently, ports and shipbuilding establishments received more than the usual attention. Many attacks were made on Emden and since this city was well defended by fighters and flak, a big air battle resulted each time the heavy bombers came over. The attack of 11 December produced an unusually fierce reaction with very large forces involved. A total of 1,088 American planes – 582 heavy bombers and 506 fighters – attacked the city. The German fighter controller apparently correctly diagnosed the objective of the mission shortly after the bombers left the English coast; as a result, the German fighters committed themselves early in the raid. Several fighter groups were jumped on their way to the bomber rendezvous while they were still flying on belly tanks. According to one comment, "the new single-engine Me-209 was encountered this raid and it out-turned, out-climbed, and out-ran our P-47 at 27,000 feet attitude."

The 3d Bomb Division, which did not have close fighter support, bore the brunt of the German attacks and suffered the heaviest losses. The Me-109 and -210's attacked the lead groups in formations of three to four abreast from high 12:00 o'clock. Eleven carried rockets were released simultaneously at the 400 yard range. Then the enemy opened up with cannon and machine guns. They came in as close as 200 yards, then dived against the low groups. These attacks were effective and are believed to have accounted for most of the total losses of seventeen bombers. Claims were 86-22-23.

The only strictly POINTBLANK operation carried out by the VIII Bomber Command during December took place on the 31st. The targets were Paris plants producing ball bearings for the German war machine and Luftwaffe depots and fields in southwestern France. Ten combat wings of the VIII Bomber Command were involved, totaling 464 effective sorties. Claims were 28-14-28 and losses were 25 bombers. Approximately 350 tons were dropped on the ball-bearing plants and the aero-engine works. The photos show wide-spread damage at all the targets. The airfields were bombed in three raids of 257, 69, and 19 aircraft. Good results were obtained, with heaviest damage being done when an oil storage dump was hit.

Although the weather interfered with operations to a considerable extent in December, the growing strength of both the Eighth and the Fifteenth Air Forces as well as the use of H2X equipment made possible a much heavier bomb load delivered than in November. Several missions of well over 400 planes were mounted by the VIII Bomber Command; approximately 12,000 tons of explosives were dropped. The Fifteenth dispatched 1,598 effective sorties, dropping some 4,300 tons. Nevertheless, POINTBLANK operations were practically nil except for the raids on Greek and Italian airdromes by XV Bomber Command. Of the some 18,000 tons dropped by both strategic air forces, only around 1,800 tons fell on POINTBLANK targets. A British source estimated that this phase of the CBO was about three months behind schedule, and the Fifteenth Air Force warned that if the offensive against the German fighter industry were not followed up by more attacks, production would reattain the July levels by February 1944.

There is no doubt that General Arnold was seriously concerned. When RAF Air Marshal Sir Trafford Leigh-Mallory visited him in November, he had been very emphatic in his demands for greater action against Luftwaffe, indeed what with our great material superiority. Although more and more bombers were being sent out and more bombs were being dropped, Arnold was not satisfied with the results. He believed there had been too many diversionary raids, especially in the case of the Eighth Air Force, against targets such as submarine pens that not contribute to the destruction of the German Air Force. In a message to the commanding generals of the Eighth and Fifteenth, he stated:

```
"It is a conceded fact that an invasion will not be possible unless the
German Air Force is destroyed. Therefore, my personal message to you —
this is a MUST —  is to DESTROY THE ENEMY AIR FORCES WHEREVER YOU FIND
HIM on the ground, in the air and HIS FACTORIES."
```

It seems likely that the slow progression of POINTBLANK also affected the decision on command problem that had been concerning the American and British staffs for some time. When the activation of a strategic air force in Italy was being considered, several plans were put forward by the American authorities to establish some sort of overall control for the various air organizations operating in Europe. Failing to convince the British of the desirability of setting up a supreme air commander for all American air forces and the RAF Bomber Command, General Arnold argued that strategic operations would be greatly facilitated if the Eighth and Fifteenth were under a unified control. This question was discussed throughout October and November with considerable opposition to the proposal coming from the British, and from Genera Eaker. Early in December, the U.S. Chiefs of Staff rejected the British objections, indicating their intentions of setting up a unified strategic control for Army air forces in the European Theater. In their memo to Combined Chiefs of Staff, the U.S. Joint Chiefs of Staff stated that "these forces should be employed primarily against POINT-BLANK objectives as the Combined Chiefs of Staff may from time to time direct." It seems reasonable to assume that General Arnold's vocal dissatisfaction with the progress of the offensive against the Germans was one of the factors that led him to favor this new arrangement.

What would ensue was a rash of new commands and a rapid shuffling of commanders. It had now been decided to reorganize the air command in the Mediterranean; on 10 December 1943, the Mediterranean Allied Air Forces (MAAF) was officially authorized. This command, under Air Marshall Sir Arthur Tedder, with Lt. Gen. Spaatz as deputy, consisted of the Fifteenth and Twelfth Air Forces, the Coastal Air Force (U.S., British, and French units), and the RAF Middle East Air Force, totaling approximately some 12,500 aircraft and 321,000 men (January 1944).

Almost immediately after the formation of MAAF, however, its command was changed. In a major reorganization of his commands, Gen. Spaatz and Air Marshall Tedder were brought to England, and General Eaker was moved from the Eighth to command MAAF with RAF Air Marshall Sir John Slessor as his deputy. These final changes were not completed until the middle of January.

The Cairo Conference of November 1943, attended by President Franklin D. Roosevelt, Prime Minister Winston Churchill, and General Chaing Kai-shek of the Republic of China, among other issues related to the war in the Pacific, sanctioned the creation of MAAF and also gave formal approval to the centralized control of strategic operations in Europe. General Arnold had long desired such control. The official directive activating the U.S. Strategic Air Forces in Europe (USSAF later USSTAF) was issued 5 January 1944. USSTAF was to come under the Supreme Allied Commander (SAC) at a future date; in the meantime, all POINTBLANK operations would be coordinated by Air Marshal Portal acting as agent of the CCS for both British and American forces. Under his direction, General Spaatz, commander of USSTAF, would direct strategic activities of the Eighth and Fifteenth Air Forces, coordinating the latter's activities as far as possible with the operations of the Allied Commander-in-Chief in the Mediterranean, Sir Harry Maitland Wilson. In case of a strategic or tactical emergency, General Wilson was empowered to use the Fifteenth Air Force as he saw fit; but for the rest, he was required to provide it full support in POINTBLANK missions, its first priority. It was soon arranged that General Spaatz would deal with the Fifteenth only through MAAF, and General Eaker would have operational control of this force subject to CBO directives.

Issuing these directives was the responsibility of Air Marshal Portal. Joint Anglo-American committees prepared studies of the various targets and presented evaluations of missions. Their recommendations finally went to the Joint Target Committee which prepared the directives for Portal's signature. The directives were received by USSTAF and then reprocessed to the Eighth and Fifteenth. General Spaatz and his deputy commander for operations, Maj. Gen. F. L. Anderson, controlled the order of selection of targets.

In some ways, the problems and duties facing the new commanding general of MAAF were much more involved than the situation in the United Kingdom had been, and it did not take General Eaker long to discover this. He wrote in March:

```
"This is a new kettle of fish from U.K. The job there was clean-cut. We
had really but one major program: to deliver the maximum bomb load against
German industry. Here we have three primary tasks and many, many
subsidiary ones. The primary tasks are: the accomplishment of POINTBLANK
with the Strategic Air Force; the support of land armies in battle with
the Tactical Air Force; and keeping the sea lanes open and protecting  the
logistic establishments with the Coastal Command. In addition, we have
such odorous morsels, or secondary commitments, as re-equipping the French,
maximum lift to the Balkan partisans, moving out of Africa and leaving the
African war behind and moving into Italy and getting on with the
continental war."
```

Furthermore, the demands of the land battle in Italy frequently cut into the strategic bombing operations. Thus, when General Eaker arrived at MAAF Headquarters, he found the Fifteenth involved in an extensive attack on airdromes in preparation for the Anzio landings on 22 January, and this continued into February. Indeed, a great deal could be written during this period about the constant tug-of-war that went on between the often conflicting demands on MAAF's vast reservoir of air power. There were conflicts between different projects; between tacticians as to whether the ground campaigns or POINTBLANK should have first call on the heavy bombers; and between the airmen as to which types of target were the best for the bombardment effort.

In spite of policy disagreements, the air war continued as intensively as the weather permitted. On 3 January, the Fifteenth raided the Fiat ball-bearing establishment at Villar-Perosa. With the successful raids on other centers of ball-bearing production such as Schweinfurt (14 October 1943) and Turin (8 November), the Fiat plant had assumed a special importance. It was reported that forty tons of ball bearings had been shipped from Italy to Germany in November; before this date, there were no comparable shipments. Furthermore, the plant at Villar-Perosa was supposed to be making a special type of bearing essential to aircraft production. Consequently, a small force of 50 B-17's attacked this target on the 3d, dropping 156 tons of 1,000-pound bombs from an altitude of 23,000 feet. The strike photos showed twelve direct hits on the main units of the plant and damaging near misses. Later reconnaissance photos showed that the factory had sustained extensive damage with twenty-five percent of the roofing destroyed.

The next missions for both the Eighth and Ninth were minor. Eighth Air Force bombers struck at the airfields at Bordeaux and Tours on the 4th, while the Fifteenth dispatched 43 heavy bombers to bomb the Steyr aero-engine factory at Maribor, Yugoslavia, on 7 January. No strike photos were obtained, and the results were not evaluated until the end of the month.

On the 8th, the Fifteenth bombed the Reggiane Aircraft Factory at Reggio Emelia, Italy. A careful reconnaissance, which indicated a considerable turnover of single-engine aircraft, preceded by mission. Between 3 and 7 January, the number of aircraft on the adjoining airfield varied from day to day as follows: 17, 23, 40, 18, and 35. It seemed likely that the Germans had converted this factory and airfield into an important depot for fighter repair, maintenance, and supply. The target was first attacked during the night of 7-8 January by 26 Wellingtons dropping 39.5 tons from 2,000 to 8,500 feet. The town, factory, and airdrome were covered with bursts; at least two 4,000-pound bombs hit the factory, with many fires started. The following day, 109 B-17's escorted by 32 P-32's dropped 324 tons on the still smoldering buildings. All opposition seemed crushed as there were no aircraft over the town and no flak. With at least twenty direct hits on the factory buildings, this target was eliminated for the time being.

The Eighth did not send out another POINTBLANK mission until 11 January when, unfortunately, weather seriously interfered. It had been planned to make an attack in force on the FW-190 assembly and component plant at Oschersleben, Germany, the Ju-88 wing manufacturing works at Halberstadt, Germany, and the aircraft assembly plants in and about

Brunswick, Germany. Over 700 bombers assembled, but unforeseen cloud formations made the mission confused and ultimately costly.

Three bombardment divisions totaling twelve combat wings were dispatched. The 1st Division consisted of 5 B-17 wings; 3 wings containing 175 bombers were to attack Oschersleben, and 2 wings containing 114 planes were sent to Halberstadt. The 3d Division made up the second formation with 134 aircraft to bomb Brunswick. The 2d Division which was flying last was to hit airplane plants at Neupetritor and Wilhelmitor, both in Germany, with 85 and 55 aircraft respectively. A total of 663 planes was dispatched.

The 1st Division took off as planned but had difficulty in contacting its full quota of escort fighters; over the last 100 miles, it was attended to by only one Mustang group which had to divide itself in two parts when the division approached its twin targets. After the 3d Division took off, the weather began to deteriorate rapidly and the formation finally received a signal ordering it to return. However, the 1st Combat Wing was near its objective and elected to continue on to the target; the other wing decided to return and bomb targets of opportunity on the way out, therby causing considerable confusion to the covering fighters. The last formation was over the Dutch coast when the recall signal was received and it turned back, bombing the towns of Meppen and Lingen, Germany on its return to England.

In spite of these difficulties, the formations that reached their targets did good work. There was some confusion among the formations of the 1st Division as the target came into view, but a good pattern was dropped on the FW-190 plant at Oschersleben. Damage was severe in the main plant area with fires burning in the machine and assembly shops. At Halberstadt, the main concentration fell just east of the plant area, but a second wave scored heavily on a large workshop and smaller buildings nearby. Good bombing was done on the factories in the Brunswick area.

Apparently, the German fighter controller first diagnosed the attacks as directed against Berlin, for virtually every German fighter within range was called into the battle, even including one enemy-flown P-38. Owing to weather and the recall of some of the wings, fighter protection for the bombers was not successful as in previous missions. As a result, some 580

German fighters were able to inflict considerable damage on the task force. The heaviest assaults came on the lead group in the 1st Division which had its low squadron entirely destroyed and lost a total of 38 planes. The combat wings of the 3d Division which penetrated to the primary target lost twelve bombers; two more were lost by the 2d during its withdrawal. Altogether, sixty heavy bombers failed to return.

#

The middle of the month brought a new operational directive for the Fifteenth from General Spaatz. The ranking objective was the destruction of the German fighter force, to be accomplished in the following order of priority:

1. GAF single-engine fighters
2. GAF twin-engine fighters
3. The ball-bearing industry

Chief targets in the first priority were the Messerschmitt factory at Regensburg; the Messerschmitt complex in Wiener Neustadt; plants in Stuttgart, Schweinfurt, and Nuremberg, Germany; and airplane factories in Austria and Hungry. However, this list remained more of a sign of things to come rather than something immediately effective. The weather, of course, frequently interfered with the long flights into Central Europe, which were necessary to reach many of these high-priority objectives. In addition to weather, the Fifteenth was unable to devote its full attention to aircraft factories because it was involved in support of the amphibious operations of the ground forces in the Rome area, which began with the landing at Anzio. Both before and during this operation, however, more than 5,000 tons of bombs were dropped by the strategic forces on aerodromes and communications. Of special importance were the attacks on eleven major airfields, which rendered the enemy reconnaissance completely ineffective and allowed the allies to achieve a rare thing in modern warfare – a complete surprise.

#

The 13th of January was a big day in counter-air force operations. As part of the preliminaries to the Anzio landing, three airfields at Perugia, Centecello and Guidonia, Italy were attacked. The Perugia airfield, a big reconnaissance center, was attacked on the night of 12-13 January by 49 Wellingtons with undetermined results. The following morning it was again struck by 40 B-17's dropping 48.9 tons of fragmentation bombs. A cloud over the target prevented an estimate of the bombing. Centecello, located on the fringes of Rome, was an important fighter base for GAF operations in support of the forces defending central Italy. It was hit by sixty-one escorted Fortresses that did some damage to service and administrative buildings. Guidonia, a little to the north, was attacked by 65 B-17's of which only 38 were able to bomb, the remainder bringing their explosives back to base. There were direct hits on a workshop, an assembly building and a transformer station. The next day, perhaps to divert the Luftwaffe's attention from central Italy, an airfield near the Yugoslav coast was raided by 140 B-17's dropping 9,638 fragmentation and 213 tons GP-bombs. Two-thirds of the field was well postholed and many installations hit.

#

This task finished, the Fifteenth was next called upon to deal with a situation at the Aviano, Italy, airfield. A reconnaissance of 26 January had revealed an increase in the number of German airplanes at this base from 54 to 72 of which 45 were now Ju-88s. It seemed that the Germans had withdrawn bombers from the Greece-Crete area for operations against the Anzio landings. Sixty-four B-17's visited this target, covering it with some 9,000 fragmentation bombs. Although German fighters took the air against the bomber formations, there were no losses. Many of the buildings on the field were hit, and the main landing area was well covered with bursts. Of the fifty-six enemy planes sighted on the field, four were damaged and one reported destroyed.

The climax of this series of tactical operations in support of the Anzio beachhead was the great counter-air force action of 30 January. The Aviano bombing was, in a sense, the prelude to this operation, for it was an attempt to break up a concentration of German low-range bombers. Following this raid, there was a wide-spread reconnaissance of German bases in northern Italy on the 28th. This showed a total of 170 enemy fighters in the area, with 127 distributed on the four fields of Maniago, Lavariano, Villaorba, and Udine, Italy. It seemed likely that the Germans were trying to counteract the threat of American bombers based in southern Italy by developing considerable air strength in the North, especially long-range bombers. For example, Villaorbawas showing a considerable increase in Ju-88's. Such bases could be used for raids against shipping and airfields in the southern area; therefore, a large operation was planned to render them useless. It was decided to bomb the four fields; however, to take care of the concentration of planes at Villaorba, this field was to be the object of a special mission planned with great skill. Since the Germans usually put all their aircraft into the air as soon as the radar informed them of the approach of heavy-bomber formations, it was decided to send a group of P-47's in below the radar screen if possible and a few minutes in advance of the heavy formations to catch the German planes still on the ground.

The surprise worked perfectly. About 1130 on the morning of the 30th, an approaching force of heavy bombers showed strong on the radar screen of the Villaorba field and the pilots began warming their motors for a quick take-off. A few had just left the ground when suddenly at 1140 a force of 60 Thunderbolt fighters swept in at terrific speed just above the treetops. The Germans were caught completely off balance, and for the next few minutes the Thunderbolts had a field day. Altogether 28 enemy planes were shot down for a loss of two. Hardly had the dust settled before 76 B-17's came sailing over at 23,000 feet to drop 10,988 frags and complete the job.

While this brilliant tour de force was being carried out at Villaorba, the three other fields were also being dealt with in summary fashion. Maniago was bombed at 1,157 by 35 B-17's, and a heavy concentration was achieved on the northern landing area. There were several fires started, with bombs seen exploding among the parked aircraft. Lavariano was attacked at the same time by forty-one heavy bombers flying in two waves. The second formation was attacked by twenty-five to thirty German fighters during the bomb run, but only one bomber was lost—the field was well covered with hits. Shortly after these three missions, sixty-three Liberators reached the Udine airfield and dropped a heavy load of fragmentation bombs. The north landing ground and hangar area were hit repeatedly, and some bursts were noted among the forty aircraft parked on the field. About 35 Me-109's and FW-190's pressed home attacks just after the bomb run was made. The bombers claimed the destruction of forteen fighters, at a loss of two Liberators.

The raids of 30 January undoubtedly dealt the enemy a severe blow. In addition to losing valuable planes, the large number of damaged aircraft probably strained his repair and maintenance facilities to the uttermost. The destruction of those facilities at Udine and Aviano made the situation even more critical. The nearest repair center now available was at Klagenfurt in Austria very near the Italian border and considered a key point in the defense of south Germany. To complete the work of the 30th, the airfields at Aviano, Udine, and Klagenfurt were attacked on the 31st by 41th, 70th, and 74th heavy bombers respectively, with successful results. At the last field, sixty-seven aircraft were seen on the ground, and eleven were destroyed and seven damaged. An estimate of the enemy air situation given in the IntelOps summary for 31 January stated the following:

```
"Experience in previous campaigns indicates that estimates of ground
damage based on photographic evidence are conservative. In the present
case, air claims appear reasonable on analysis of the apparently
serviceable aircraft remaining after the attacks. Concrete evidence shows
at least 145enemy aircraft destroyed or damaged and it is highly probable
that substantially more were rendered unserviceable by the operation."
```

Eighth Air Force operations during this same period were against other than POINTBLANK targets. Weather in many cases prevented the deep penetrations necessary to reach centers of GAF production, and blind-bombing equipment worked more successfully against harbors and port installations than against the small towns where some of the factories were located. The only major mission of the month against an aircraft factory turned out to be unsuccessful. Out of an available strength of 918 bombers, 777 were dispatched on the 30th to attack the factories in the Brunswick area. Unfortunately weather conditions proved very bad with 10/10 cloud over the entire Continent with tops reaching up as high as 27,000 feet. The 14th Combat Wing lost contact with the other formations and bombed Hanover instead of the primary. No estimates of the bombing could be given because all formations bombed by radar equipment. The German fighter opposition was strong, with approximately 300 fighters involved. Rockets were used successfully. In spite of escort fighters numbering 635, 20 bombers were lost, and 4 fighters. The fighters claimed 45-15-34.

A new phase of air warfare was introduced on the 31st when 75 fighter-bombers of the VIII Fighter Command were dispatched with an escort to dive-bomb the Gilze-Rijen airdrome in Holland. A total of 17.5 tons were so dropped, and as the weather was generally clear in the area, the results were good. Approximately 120 enemy aircraft opposed the operation and some vicious combats took place. Six escorting fighters were shot down; in return, the Eighth's fighters claimed enemy losses at 13-0-1.

On the whole, January like December was not an important month for POINTBLANK operations. Both bad weather and obligations to support the ground battle handicapped the Fifteenth. Nevertheless, its extensive attacks on German airfields, while dictated by the current tactical situation, were in keeping with General Arnold's orders to strike the Luftwaffe on the ground and in the air, and should be counted as a phase of POINTBLANK. This air force counted 3,802 effective bomber sorties for the relatively low loss of 64 heavy bombers. A total of 11,051 tons of bombs were dropped on all targets, and fighter and bomber claims of enemy planes destroyed came to 320.

The Eighth Air Force was likewise handicapped by the ever-present problem of weather. Although not involved in supporting a land battle, its program of operations was somewhat thrown off balance by the appearance of new and totally unexpected targets with a high priority. These were the German robot-plane installations, at first known as "construction works", later as NOBALL targets, and later to be known as V-1 and V-2 launch sites, which began to stud the Channel coast of France late in 1943. Although there had been a few exploratory raids in the autumn, really serious attacks did not begin until December. From that month until the end of March, both the Eighth and Ninth Air Forces were forced to deliver repeated attacks against these menacing institutions. Thus, the NOBALL targets combined with weather to make POINTBLANK operations difficult. The Ninth Air Force, for example, was so occupied with missions against NOBALL that it was able to bomb only one airfield, that at Cherbourg/ Maupertus, which was hit twice as a secondary target on 7 January.

In spite of their losses, the Luftwaffe was still able to make a vigorous defense of targets it considered vital. On some occasions, deep penetrations were opposed by as many as 385 fighter planes; nearly all the important missions were met by at least 100 fighters. It was evident that the enemy was still experimenting with all kinds of aerial weapons in the hopes of meeting the attacks on his industries. Aerial bombs, glide bombs, parachute bombs and even bombs on cables were used at one time or another against our formations. Rockets were constantly fired by enemy planes during the air battles, and were responsible for a good many losses. Nevertheless, our wastage remained relatively low; the 203 bombers destroyed in January were only 4.3 percent of the effective sorties. Against this loss, the VIII Bomber Command dropped 12,397 tons, with claims of 582-156-129. If the Fighter Command's claims are added to these figures, we get the overall claim of 795 German planes of all types destroyed during January. However, there is strong reason for believing these claims were unduly high, and General Doolittle once stated as much, urging his lower-echelon commanders to see that all figures were as accurate as possible.

The CBO was now into its fourth phase, according to the original schedule. It had been assumed that by 1944, air operations would be designed to prepare for the coming invasion of the Continent and that the Luftwaffe would not be a serious threat. But in January the Luftwaffe was still very much of a threat. An CCS study estimated the Me-109 program was seven months behind schedule and the FW-190 was four; nevertheless, the Air Ministry's figures showed an increase of 50 single-engine planes over the December production figures. If the weather during February continued to prevent deep penetrations of the Reich, perhaps the German aircraft production would again reach the high figures of July 1943.

On the 24th of January, General Arnold discussed the situation in a letter to General Spaatz. He was concerned over the small number of bombers being sent to destroy important targets, and feared our air superiority was being divided up into small forces assigned to targets all over Europe: "Can't we, some day and not too far distant send out a big number - and I mean a big number - of bombers to hit something in the nature of an aircraft factory and lay it flat?" The answer to this question was to come in the raids of 20-25 February, the famous "Big Week" of the U. S. Army Air Forces.

5

THE BIG WEEK AND ITS BACKGROUND

At the end of January, the Air Ministry estimates of GAF monthly production were as follows:

S/E fighters	650
T/E fighters	190
LR bombers and Reconnaissance	315

Following the February attacks, especially the period from the 20th through the 25th, known as the Big Week, the Air Ministry estimates indicated a drop in production to these figures:

S/E fighters	245
T/E fighters	55
LR bombers and Reconnaissance	210

This achievement was the result of the heaviest bomber attacks yet mounted in the air war, plus the determination of General Spaatz to press home the offensive against the Luftwaffe. In a letter of 23 January 1944 to

Robert A. Lovett, Assistant Secretary of War for Air, he stated his bombing plans:

"I believe …that the ability to apply the pressure from two sides against the middle can be utilized to the discomfiture of the enemy. My tendency will be to place a little bit more emphasis upon swatting the enemy on his airdromes whenever possible, and force him to fight under conditions most advantageous to us. There are certain essential targets, however, such as fighter factories and ball-bearing works, beyond fighter cover, which must be hit when weather conditions permit accurate bombing results. These attacks will no doubt result in heavy losses, but will materially reduce our later losses."

Shortly after, the Air Ministry issued a comprehensive bombardment program for the Eighth, Fifteenth, and British bomber commands. First and equal priority was to go to single-engine and twin-engine fighter airframe and component production. The Eighth Air Force's targets were listed in the following order:

1. Erla Me-109 plant at Leipzig
2. Me-109 plant at Regensburg/Prufening(also the Fifteenth)
3. FW-190 plant at Rosen
4. Me-110 plant at Gotha
5. Ju-88 plants at Bernburg, Halberstadt, and Oschersleben, Germany
6. Me-110 plant at Brunswick
7. FW-190 assembly at Tutow, Germany
8. FW-190 assembly at Kassel
9. Ju-88 plant at Schkeuditz, Germany

For the Fifteenth Air Force the first priority air production centers were:

1. Me-109 plant at Regensburg/Prufening
2. Me-410 assembly plant at Augsburg, Germany
3. The components plant at Styr
4. The Me-109 plant at Fischamend, Austria
5. The Me-410 plant in Szigetszentmiklos, Hungry
6. Me-110 plant at Brunswick

The RAF was accorded first priority to the following industrial cities: Schweinfurt, Leipzig, Brunswick, Regensburg, Augsburg and Gotha. When weather was unsuitable for priority objectives, both the RAF Bomber Command and the Eighth Air Force were to attack Berlin if conditions permitted. Ball-bearing plants were also given an equal priority with aircraft establishments.

With the question of bombing policy and targets settled, other problems were to be handled. In order to enable both bomber crews and fighter pilots to understand each other's problems, a fighter liaison officer was henceforth to be sent to each bombardment division in the Eighth Air Force. At the same time, the VIII Fighter Command prepared a memo on the tactics and techniques of fighter escort—this was to serve as a guide, not only for the liaison officer but also for staff officers of the bombardment divisions. When unusual problems were discussed which might concern fighters as well as bombers, fighter personnel were to attend the operational critiques held at bomber command headquarters. From then on, fighter command intelligence was to receive more information from the bomber crews as to where and when the heaviest attacks came, what were the enemy tactics, and so on. It was hoped that in this way closer coordination between bomber and fighter groups might be achieved, and more effective escort missions be flown.

The question of claims, so often the object of criticism by both British and American authorities, came up again during February. As General Doolittle admitted, Eighth Air Force air-to-air claims undoubtedly had been high. In an effort to avoid duplicate claims, a new system for recording them was developed and sent to the lower echelons; h owever, it is not certain that much was accomplished. Because of the close formations flown by the heavy bombers, German fighters shot down were almost always the target of several gunners. In this connection, it is interesting to point out that after Herman Goering was captured, he stated our claims were usually about three times the actual losses. According to the former chief of the Luftwaffe, the heaviest loss in fighter pilots was on 1 January 1945, when approximately 100 pilots were shot down. In spite of all efforts, claims continued to be difficult to evaluate throughout the war.

The first part of February was, as General Spaatz had indicated, largely given over to attacks on German airfields. On the 5th, the Eighth went on a big sweep of five GAF training bases and one assembly and repair depot. Every target was in France. A total of 509 bombers, from an available effective strength of 855, was dispatched to Chateauroux, Orleans/Pricey, Tours, Alvord, and Chateaudun. Romilly-sur-Seine had originally been included in the target list, but since it was covered with cloud, the repair depot at Villacoublay was bombed instead. Some 1,200 tons were dropped with excellent or good results at all targets except Chateaudun where results were estimated as fair. Only two bombers and two fighters were lost, with total claims at 16-5-6.

On the 6th, the Eighth was out again in force. This time 642 heavies were sent to strike targets in the Pas de Calais area, but found it covered by 10/10 cloud; consequently, eight targets of opportunity were bombed instead. Among these were the airfields at Chateaudun, Evreux/Fauville, and Caen/Carpiquet. The VIII Fighter Command and the RAF provided 632 escorts.

Two days later, the Fifteenth attacked the airdromes at Viterbo, Tarquina, and Orvieto in Italy with small task forces. Of the forty-four aircraft present at Viterbo, six were probably destroyed and four damaged. All three fields were in central Italy a short distance north of Rome, and all were in fighter range of the beleaguered Anzio beachhead.

On the 10th, the Eighth scheduled a mission to attack targets in the Brunswick area and also the Gilze-Rijen airdrome in Holland. However, adverse weather and the failure of the radar equipment interfered with the eighty-one Liberators dispatched to the aerodrome and only twenty-seven attacked. Unfortunately, two mid-air collisions occurred, causing the loss of three B-24's. The 189 Flying Fortresses sent to Brunswick experienced some weather trouble, but two of the three wings found holes in the overcast and were able to drop their bombs visually. Strike photos indicated the 350 tons of bombs covered the area of the old town with good results, although it was not possible to tell if the aircraft establishments had been hit. It had been hoped that the attack on Gilze-Rijen would cause the Germans to divert some of the fighter force in this direction; unfortunately, the GAF was not deceived. Furthermore, bad weather caused the withdrawal escorts to be delayed in meeting the formations, and two groups completely missed the rendezvous; this gave the Luftwaffe its opportunity. About 350 fighters attacked the bomber formations. Contrails were exceptionally heavy, affording the enemy an excellent cover from which to make sudden strikes. Our claims were 55-2-42, but the cost was high; 8 fighters and 29 bombers were destroyed.

The 218th operation on the 11th, although not directed at a POINT-BLANK target, is of considerable interest because of what looked like a possible change in GAF tactics. Heretofore, it had been sometimes difficult for our fighters to get the German fighters to engage them. The GAF usually preferred to keep away from the Mustangs, Thunderbolts and Lightnings in order to concentrate on the bombers; however, the opposite technique was followed in this mission. The Germans abandoned their usual tactics and turned viciously on the fighters. Several sharp engagements took place; as a result, the American escorts claimed 32-3-22 but lost 14 of their own number - a high figure for fighters. In addition, 4 P-47's, 2 P-38's and 1 P-51 were seriously damaged. When General Arnold received this information, he was quick to see the possibility of a change in GAF tactics. He cabled General Spaatz to inquire if our fighters were going to abandon their escort functions to take aggressive action against German fighters whenever encountered. Replying for General Spaatz, General Anderson stated they welcomed this aggressive action against the fighters as it permitted them to restore considerable freedom of action to our escorts who would now be able to force the Germans into combat. As it turned out, this did not mark the beginning of a new policy, and other missions found the Luftwaffe none too anxious to engage the Thunderbolts and Mustangs, preferring instead to save ammunition and gasoline for the big formations of heavy bombers.

Certainly these operations were not the "big numbers" of bombers out to lay something "flat" that General Arnold had been hoping for. Nevertheless, such an operation involving both the Eighth and Fifteenth Air Forces had been scheduled for some time. One of the principal motives in the activation of the Fifteenth had been the hope that the two strategic bombing forces could coordinate their joint operations. It was confidently expected that the Po Valley would soon be available for Anglo-American air bases and that the Fifteenth "and the Eighth would integrate their attacks on German targets with frequent joint raids, shuttles, one-two punches, etc." The Po

Valley remained in enemy hands. But in early December a plan for a combined attack on the German aircraft industry was being drawn up under the code name of ARGUMENT. It is not clear if this operation was actually planned for 1943, although one writer suggests that it was first scheduled for 12 December but supply deficiencies and weather had forced a cancellation.

ARGUMENT was definitely scheduled for January, and it was hoped that weather conditions on the 15th might be suitable for combined operations, but the plans had to be canceled. Fog closed down the English bases and storms lay along the air routes beyond the Alps. On the 26th, General Spaatz cabled General Arnold that he had been going into the weather situation carefully with Anderson, Doolittle, LeMay, Hodges and Williams. He felt that unless some frequency of operation could be maintained and increased pressure applied to the "Hun Air Force," necessary wastage would not be obtained.

Hoping that February might provide the opportunity for this increased pressure, USSTAF set up an elaborate system for coordinating operations on the 3d. Coordinated actions might be instituted by either air force, or they could be brought about by the Combined Operational Planning Committee. The commanding general of USSTAF could also order a combined operation, which only he could cancel, except in the case of an extreme emergency in the land battle in Italy when the theater commander could commandeer bomber support for his ground troops.

Another combined operation was ordered for the 9th as there seemed a chance that the weather might be favorable. Some 843 heavy bombers were actually dispatched by the Eighth, but were recalled before they had crossed the English coast. The Fifteenth was held down by inoperative bases and deteriorating weather conditions along the route and consequently its bombers did not take to the air. General Eaker wrote to General Spaatz that he was "most disappointed that our joint plan for operation was again messed up by the weather last night and today. One day we shall get on with that job. I am personally certain there has been no decent day for it since last August 18th. That is almost unbelievable but nevertheless true."

Meanwhile in the United Kingdom, Maj. Gen. F. L. Anderson, Spaatz's deputy for operations, was still hopeful that a few good days might be vouchsafed to them, although his weather experts cheerfully assured him that the chances were 8 to 1 against it. In spite of this dubious prediction, on the 11th he wrote to General Laurence S. Kuter, one of the authors of AFWD/1 and currently on the air war planning staff in Washington, D.C., that he was "now in the midst of preparing a plan which will best exploit the destruction of the aircraft and ball-bearing factories." His confidence was justified. The atmospheric conditions took a turn for the better; on the 17th, Anderson was informed that a stretch of relatively good weather seemed to be shaping up. With this long-awaited gift of fortune almost in his hands, General Spaatz began to set in motion the machinery for a combined offensive by the Eighth and Fifteenth, when suddenly a new obstacle appeared.

As this study has already pointed out, the directive, which provided for the control of the Fifteenth, permitted the theater commander to make use of the strategic air arm in case of an emergency. The battle at the Anzio beachhead, which had been going on since 22 January, was reaching a climax. On the night of 15-16 February, the Germans launched a heavy counterattack with intensive air and artillery preparation. The situation was critical, and General Mark C. Clark, commanding General of the Fifth Army in Italy, and Maj. Gen. John K. Cannon of the tactical air force felt the need of assistance from the heavy bombers of the strategic force. This was of course the possibility foreseen in the directive giving many months before to Allied Commander-in-Chief of the Mediterranean General Harry Wilson when received the authority to temporarily withdraw the Fifteenth from POINTBLANK to assist in the land attack. Nevertheless, General Eaker, for the sake of precedent, wished to prevent a situation where an official demarche by General Wilson would be necessary. Consequently, when it was apparent that a combined operation was to take place on the 20th, General Eaker signaled Spaatz on their private wire as follows:

"Re your mission assignment to Fifteenth for tomorrow, here is our situation: (a) Clark and Cannon believe tomorrow will be critical day in beachhead: both hope for full heavy bomber help. Cannon believes some heavies must help. (b) Our weather prophets believe we have little chance for visual targets in South Germany. You speak of area targets. We have no H2X as you know. In view of foregoing, we face this problem: Shall General Wilson declare emergency under CCS directive and employ heavies. I hope to avoid this. Will you therefore tell me as soon as possible whether your other planned attacks require our help as diversion even with no prospect of visual bombing. In that event we must make a split and send five or six groups on one or two targets you name and put

at least four on beachhead support. In view of our dilemma, please give
me desires."

General Spaatz immediately gave Eaker a release from the combined
operation, but he was concerned for fear a continuous emergency at the
beachhead might interfere with POINTBLANK. During the next two or
three days, the favorable weather conditions, which had been so anxiously
awaited for almost three months, might occur. Consequently, although he
appreciated the emergency conditions at the beachhead and was willing to
release the Fifteenth from participation in the POINTBLANK operation
scheduled for the 20th, he hoped nothing "would prevent heavy force of Fifteenth Air Force from being utilized against POINTBLANK targets
Monday and Tuesday (21 and 22 February) if weather permits."

In this way the power of the Fifteenth was made available to the ground
forces without the necessity of General Wilson's intervention under the pro-
visions of the CCS directive. In fact, such action was never necessary
because this procedure set the pattern for the future. There were at least six
occasions when the effort of the heavy bombers was swung to the side of the
ground forces; on each occasion, the cooperation was secured on a request
basis. As a result of the arrangement with General Spaatz, the Fifteenth dispatched 105 bombers to the beachhead on the 20th, while another force of
126 attempted to reach Regensburg but was prevented by the weather
which, in south Germany at least, failed to live up to expectations. It was not
until the 22nd that a combined operation was possible.

Meanwhile, the Eighth Air Force was preparing to take advantage of the
clearing weather promised for the 20th. Since the targets to be bombed lay
in central and eastern Germany, the RAF coordinated its night bombing
with AAF plans by hitting Leipzig and Berlin during the night of 19-20 February. At that time the weather forecast indicated relatively favorable
weather conditions: small, low clouds were predicted for central Germany,
nil to 3/10 cloud for eastern and 6/10 to 8/10 low cloud for northern Germany.

Therefore, it was decided to send out the heaviest possible force against
some 12 targets connected with the production of the Me-109, Me-110,
Ju-88, Ju-188, and the FW-190. The FW facilities at Kreising, Poland, and

Posen (Pozan), Poland and Tutow in northern Germany were one general objective, and in the Leipzig/Brunswick area the targets included the Leipzig-Mockau airfield, the Erla Messerschmitt factory, the Junkers repair and assembly plant, the Erla machine works at Heiterblick and Abtnaundorf, the Junkers airframe and engine works at Aschersleben, Halberstadt, and Bernburg, the Me-110 components factories in the Wilhelmitor and Neupetritor suburbs of Brunswick, and the Gothaer Waggonfabrik aircraft plant at Gotha, a component and assembly plant for the Me-110.

Plans for the mission were very carefully worked out. The heaviest weight of the attack was to fall on the Leipzig/Brunswick targets, with the force dispatched to the Posen/Tutow area acting as a diversion on the flank. The routes were chosen to deceive the enemy as long as possible concerning the real objectives, and to make it appear as though Berlin might be the destination. The approach to the Posen targets was to be a wide swing to the north over Denmark just about the same time that the main task force to the south would be entering the enemy's radar screen. This was to prevent the enemy controller from dispatching his full fighter strength against the flanking attack from the north, and also to force him to split his forces. It was also planned that the Fifteenth should come up from the south to strike at Regensburg, but it has already been pointed out that weather and other commitments interfered.

At 0930 on 20 February, the first formations took off on what was then the largest force of bombers ever deployed on a daylight mission. Participating were 12 combat wings totaling 1,003 bombers. To protect this tremendous force, RAF and American fighters flew 832 sorties. This was the "really big" mission that General Arnold had been hoping for, and it was out to lay the German aircraft industry "flat."

The flanking diversionary forces found the weather not as good as had been expected. Tutow sits overcast and the bombers used blind-bombing techniques or attacked targets of opportunity. There was no observation of results. Finding the overcast equally as heavy at Posen and Kreising, the planes decided to bomb Rostock as a target of opportunity, dropping 196.5 tons of HE and 121.8 tons of IB. Considerable damage was done to the Neptunwerk shipyard, and the Ernest Heinkel airframe and assembly factory at Marienehe all in Rostock. Though this was not the major part of the operation, considerable fighter opposition developed. (It would later be known that the development of the first German jet fighter was taking place in Rostock.)

Ten combat wings comprised the main task force which was dispatched into central Germany. The routes were flown almost as briefed with good fighter cover. From the behavior of the German fighter controller, it appears evident that the enemy was completely outwitted by the diversion to the north. This northern force was apparently considered to be the main thrust and a large force of GAF fighters was dispatched to intercept it "while the controller who had launched it looked anxiously over his left shoulder at another large bomber force which was approaching the Reich across Holland." Suddenly, he decided that the southern force was the main attack and ordered his fighters to return to the Hanover area. This was a fundamental mistake, for it brought the enemy interceptors back too late to oppose the bomber formations en route to the objectives; as a result, the enemy was never able to oppose this operation in force.

As the bombers approached the target area, the undercast broke up and visual bombing was possible. The Leipzig/Mockau airfield and the Erla Messerschmitt factory were attacked by 131 aircraft dropping 281.8 tons of HE bombs and 85.2 tons of incendiaries. Three aircraft factories bordering the field received extensive damage and there were direct hits on the assembly shop of the Erla plant and nearby hangars. The transport-bomber assembly factory was covered with a heavy concentration, with some Junkers installations damaged.

At Heiterblick near Leipzig, the weight of the attack fell on the power houses and workshops as seventy-five bombers dropped high explosive and incendiaries. At Bernburg the Junkers airframe and aero-engine centers were assaulted by a small force of thirty-seven planes, but the bombardiers were able to achieve hits on factory buildings and probably did blast damage to a fuselage storage building. At Brunswick both the Neupetritor and Wilhelmitor suburbs were successfully bombed and direct hits were scored on Me-110 component manufacturing installations at the former. Due to the overcast, the Gothaer Waggonfabrik was attacked by eighty-nine bombers using blind-bombing techniques; the results were not immediately observable. Targets of opportunity were also hit at Oschersleben and Strassfurt, Germany, with fair to good results.

This operation of the 20th was later adjudged one of the most successful ever carried out of this air force. German fighter defense was far below what was expected. Uncertainty as to the destination of the bombers may have contributed to this weakness, as well as the weather over Holland and the possible exhaustion of the night fighters as a result of the heavy night attack on Leipzig which kept the German pilots flying until 0450. The total losses were twenty-one bombers and four fighters. The claims of both bombers and fighters were tentatively set at 123-40-66.

The next day the weather began to deteriorate; the forecast for central and northwest Germany was 5/10 to 7/10 cloud coverage at low level with large breaks. Under such circumstances there was a good chance for some clear targets; consequently, some 800 planes were dispatched against two aircraft factories, six major airfields, and aircraft storage areas in western Germany. The Brunswick targets and the fields and targets at Diepholz were bombed, but the weather interfered at the others; as a result, numerous targets of opportunity were bombed, including seven other airfields. Not all formations were properly organized and not all target areas were reached. The third combat wing was originally assigned to the Brunswick targets but initially followed the second air wing to Diepholz and were far off route before the error was noticed. Consequently, this wing decided to bomb the airfields at Neinburg and Verden as targets of opportunity. Varying degrees of damage was inflicted on the airfields.

At Diepholz four storage buildings and the workshops were destroyed, with major damage done to hangars and barracks. A direct hit on an ammunition dump was achieved, and a severe explosion followed. The bombing at Brunswick was hard to evaluate since it was carried out with radar equipment, but it was believed most of the bombs fell in the core of the city.

The GAF reaction was somewhat slow in developing. Some 150 enemy aircraft were airborne but did not attack until the bombers reached the target area. Unfavorable weather conditions may have hampered the Luftwaffe, but it was also believed the German fighter defenses were beginning to show the strain which these large-scale operations put upon them. The B-26 bombers of the IX Bomber Command attacked enemy airfields and

caused some fighters to become airborne prematurely. The RAF also contributed its share by attacking Stuttgart 12 hours before the 8th began its
operations. American claims were only 19-18-14, and the loss of 16
bombers out of a total of 861 airborne was not considered heavy. Although
the weather did not hold up as well as had been expected, General Spaatz
cabled General Arnold that he was well pleased with the results of the battle
so far. Full pressure was being maintained on the enemy air force, and he
was to be allowed no time for recuperation even if it meant some extra
American losses due to weather.

The forecast for the 22nd indicated that southwest France and parts of
Germany would be clear; it also seemed possible that the air routes over the
Alps would be open and that the Fifteenth could at last take part in the Big
Week. For the third successive day of this massive attack on the Luftwaffe
and its sources of supply, six high-priority CBO targets were selected: (1)
the Junkers plant at Halberstadt, makers of wings for Ju-88 and -188; (2)
the Junkers aircraft components and final assembly at Oschersleben; (3)
the Gothaer components and final assembly of the FW-190 at Oschersleben; (4) the Junkers assembly at Bernburg; (5) the ball-bearing factory at
Schweinfurt; and (6) the Gothaer component and assembly plant for the
Me-110 at Gotha, the largest producer of twin-engine fighters. In addition,
the Fifteenth was scheduled to bomb the aircraft factories at Regensburg.

To deceive the German fighter control, one combat wing was ordered to
attack the Aalborg airfield in north Denmark as a diversionary mission.
This force was the first to use aircraft equipped with Mandrel, a device to
jam the enemy Freya, Chimney, Hoarding, and Wurzburg radar sets. Using
their jammers, it was hoped the Mandrel planes of this force could deny the
Germans the use of their own radar to detect the approach of the main task
force. It was also hoped that the diversionary force would hold down a considerable number of German fighter units of the Helgeland area of Denmark
and prevent their joining with other groups in the defense of central Germany.

These elaborate plans were not too successful. Weather prevented the
fifty-eight bombers of the diversionary task force from bombing the Aalborg
field, and the German fighters were not diverted from the main effort. However, in the opinion of some experts, the Fifteenth's attack on Regensburg

may have attracted twin-engine fighters that otherwise might have been used against the Eighth's formations. Fourteen combat wings constituted the main effort of the VIII Bomber Command. In the first wave were 289 B-17's headed for Halberstadt, Aschersleben, Bernburg, and Oschersleben; the second formation consisted of 333 B-17's assigned to attack Schweinfurt; and the third and final wave was made up of 253 B-24's bound for Gotha.

Trouble was encountered from the very beginning. Clouds, snow, haze, and stronger-than-predicted winds considerable disturbed the assembling formations. Some wings managed to get into some sort of order by the time the coast of Holland was reached, but others did not and were forced to abort. The 2d bomb division was unable to organize; after penetrating about 100 miles inland, it decided to abandon the Gotha mission and bomb targets of opportunity. Unfortunately, the bombardiers did not allot sufficiently for the strong wind and four Dutch towns were bombed by mistake. Of the 455 bombers actually dispatched, 101 attacked the primary targets and 154 bombed targets of opportunity. Thirty-four aircraft reached Aschersleben, dropping 64.5 tons of high explosives and 12.6 tons of incendiaries on the Junkers factory. The concentration on the target was good; it was estimated that the damage was extensive; six large workshops received direct hits.

The Junkers factory at Bernburg was hit successfully by 45 bombers and 45 tons of GP and 64.9 tons of fragmentation bombs. Only 18 airplanes managed to reach the Halberstadt installations, and photographic cover failed to show any hits on the Junkers factory, although 49.5 tons were dropped. The formations headed for Oschersleben bombed targets of opportunity with generally poor results.

For the first time during the three days of continuous operations against the German fighter industry, the Luftwaffe reacted vigorously. For one thing, they had an excellent opportunity to inflict considerable damage. As has been pointed out, the bad weather upset the formations and generally scrambled the timetable and over-all plans. Since many of the groups were looking for targets of opportunity, the schedule for the withdrawal was not adhered to. All this made it very difficult for the escort fighters to have proper support and coverage especially since they were outnumbered by the

German fighters frequently. In addition, some of the bombers elected to return along courses north of the planned route; this gave the Ruhr defense system time to engage them. All these factors made the mission a costly one; eleven fighters and forty-one bombers were lost. The bombers claimed 27-3-31, and the fighters claimed 60-7-25.

Meanwhile, the Fifteenth force had at last been able to get its planes into southern Germany. While the Eighth was struggling with weather and the Luftwaffe, the Fifteenth was attacking the great Messerschmitt complex at Regensburg. Sixty-five Flying Fortresses dropped 153 tons of high explosive and incendiary bombs on the Messerschmitt factory; weather prevented an accurate appraisal of the bombing. At the same time, 118 Liberators attacked the aircraft factory at Regensburg/Obertraubling with GP and incendiary bombs. Here again, poor photos and bad weather prevented an estimate of the results, although visual observations during the attack indicated that the target area was hit—and one considerable explosion was noted. At the same time, 28 unescorted B-17's dropped 81 tons of 500-lb. GP bombs on the Zagreb (Yugoslavia) airdrome with fair results.

Although the operations of 22 February were not among the most successful of the so-called Big Week, they are of special interest because of the fact that both the Eighth and the Fifteenth were able to run coordinated missions. Those who have struggled along with the author of this study so far will recall that one of the arguments for the creation of the Fifteenth Air Force was based on the idea of combined operations with the Eighth. Nevertheless, bad weather and the demands of the land battle in Italy made such coordination relatively rare. In this particular case, it is not clear whether or not the combination was of much assistance to either force. The heavy losses of the Eighth do not appear to have been greatly affected by the attack on Regensburg or the Zagreb airdrome; nor was the operation against the Regensburg factories of sufficient weight to divert many of the fighter groups from central Germany. The one-two punch against the German aircraft industry by both the strategic air forces was still something to be worked out in the future.

The 23rd of February found bad weather settling down on the British Isles and no operations took place. The Fifteenth sent 102 Liberators to the Steyrwaffen Walzlagerwerk at Steyr, Austria, where they dropped 214 tons of bombs without much success, according to the photos showing no serious damage to any vital installation. The GAF reacted vigorously to this mission and aggressive attacks were launched against the formations for about thirty minutes. Seven Liberators were seen shot down and ten more were missing when the bombers returned to their bases. The Fifteenth did not stage any more attacks due to the bad weather.

By the morning of the 24th, climatic conditions had greatly improved, and nil to 3/10 low cloud was promised for most continental areas. Selecting its targets in furtherance of the over-all plan for the destruction of the German aircraft industry, the Eighth scheduled something like a repetition of the first mission of the Big Week. The targets were the VHF Werke I at Schweinfurt, already heavily damaged in prior raids, the Gothaer Waggonfabrik at Gotha, and a northern diversionary raid on the aircraft assembly plants at Tutow, Posen, and Kreising, plus a feint over the North Sea.

Elaborate precautions were taken to confuse the GAF fighters. The Tutow-Posen-Kreising task force was to leave one hour and fifteen minutes before the rest so as to bring the main force into the enemy radar screen as late as possible and not discourage the bulk of the German fighters from attacking the weaker northern forces. On the other hand, it was hoped the late commitment of the main formations would not give the enemy time to recall his fighter groups north toward the Tutow-Posen-Kreising nexus. The diversionary force dispatched over the North Sea was not intended to bomb anything, but it had the two-fold task of jamming the enemy's radar with its Mandrel planes and drawing some units of the Luftwaffe away from the target areas. If the timing could be carried out properly, the enemy units attacking the diversionary forces would need refueling about the time the bombers assigned to Schweinfurt and Gotha would be crossing the coast of Holland. A further trick to confuse the German fighter control was the fact that the forces going into northern Germany were so routed as to appear headed for Berlin. The withdrawal routes were plotted south of the Ruhr to pull the GAF away from the retiring northern forces.

Unfortunately, the behavior of the weather did not fit into these elaborate plans. When the Posen-Tutow-Kreising task force reached the target area, it was found to be completely overcast. Therefore, it was decided to bomb Rostock instead, as 236 aircraft dropped 560.6 tons of high explosive and incendiary bombs. Owing to the smoke reconnaissance photos were not available. Sixty-one bombers dropped 156.3 tons prematurely on an unidentified point east of the target with undisclosed results. The diversionary force over the North Sea flew its mission without incident; it does not appear to have deceived the Germans.

Meanwhile, the main forces were proceeding toward their objectives. The Schweinfurt force consisted of 266 Fortresses, while 238 Liberators were assigned to bomb Gotha. At Schweinfurt some 574.3 tons were dropped on the ball-bearing plants with excellent results. Three out of four of the factories sustained major damage, and there were additional hits on machine shops, storage buildings, and power stations. The tonnage on Gotha was not as heavy as had been expected owing to the fact that 44 B-24's dropped 107.4 tons on Eisenach by mistake. The remaining 171 Liberators found the proper target and covered it with 421.1 tons of incendiaries and high explosives. The Gothaer Waggonfabrik lost four large workshops, while three others and several medium workshops were damaged. In a nearby GAF airfield a heavy concentration of bursts covered the field, barracks, and administration buildings.

In spite of a large fighter cover—801 fighters were airborne, and 767 sorties were flown—the bomber losses were the heaviest of the Big Week. For one thing, an unexpectedly strong tail wind brought the lead groups into the target area ahead of schedule and carried them away from their escorts at times. GAF opposition was moderate in the Schweinfurt area, and only eleven bombers were lost there; howveer, the defense was stubborn and intense at Gotha. As the Liberators retired from the area, they were subjected to heavy attacks, apparently because they were flying at a considerably lower altitude than the B-17's. A total of 33 B-24's was lost on the Gotha mission, and losses for the entire operation came to 49 bombers and 10 fighters. The heavies claimed 79-9-31 enemy losses, and fighter claims were 37-5-14.

The Fifteenth Air Force was also operational on the 24th. The target was the Steyr-Daimler-Puch aircraft factory at Steyr, Austria. Eighty-seven B-17's dropped 261 tons of 500 lb. GP bombs in the target area. Several of the machine shops were badly damaged, one building receiving twelve direct hits, another six, and a third had one. In the main part of the factory, three direct hits landed on the machine shops, two were scored on assemblies and one on the vehicle assembly shop. About 110 enemy aircraft of all types subjected the Fifteenth's bombers to an hour's heavy attack. Rockets and aerial bombs were employed, and 16 B-17's, 2 P-38's, and 1 P-47 were destroyed. The attacks seemed to be concentrated on the rear formations; the 2d Bomb Group flying in that position lost ten planes. American claims against the GAF were 35-12-5.

During the hours following this double operation by the Eighth and Fifteenth, the weather continued to improve, and the RAF was able to visit Schweinfurt on the night of the 24th in the wake of the Eighth's successful mission a few hours before. In view of the heavy strain being imposed on the Luftwaffe, and the weather forecast of generally clear for inland continental areas on 25 February, General Spaatz decided to mount another attack in great strength against German aircraft production. Both the strategic air forces were assigned to batter the great Me-109 complex at Regensburg; in addition, the Eighth was to attack Messerschmitt parent plant and research center at Augsburg, the ball-bearing factory at Stuttgart, and the Me-110 component and assembly plant at Furth. As in the two previous air battles, a small Mandrel force was to operate against the German radar from the North Sea.

The first phase of the highly successful operations on the 25th was carried out by the Fifteenth Air Force. Striking north from Italian bases, 46 B-17's and 103 B-24's headed for Regensburg, escorted by 36 P-47's and 65 P-38s. Just as this task force was crossing the northern tip of the Adriatic, they sighted vapor trails 4,000 to 5,000 feet ahead and above the formations, and realized that the Luftwaffe was waiting for them. Attacks began immediately and continued for one hour and thirty minutes without interruption. The original attacking force probably came from Graz, Austria; as the battle developed, replacements moved in from Klagenfurt, Austria. As in the mission of 24 February, the rear groups were subjected to the hottest part of the assault:

"The lead elements of the rear groups were jumped by single-engine fighters attacking in threes-in-line astern, or sometimes in line abreast, from ahead, head on and below …twin-engine fighters in formations of ten in line abreast, echelons four or five deep were observed. Rear

echelons attacked in successive waves laying down a barrage of cannon
fire on a specific element of the bomber formation. It appeared that at
least 1 B-17 was lost to each pass."

In spite of this fierce opposition, the bombers reached the Regensburg/
Prufening aircraft factory and inflicted great injury on it. Photos showed at
least twenty-four direct hits and nineteen near misses on the final assembly
shop, and on the component erection shop for wings and fuselages. Many
fires were burning as the bombers left the area. American losses were thirty-
nine bombers.

While this operation was being carried out, 780 heavy bombers of the
Eighth were moving through the air toward their various targets. The routes
were flown approximately as planned. A towering wind caused many of the
formations to slip on their timetable; consequently, some of the lead elements were without escort support as they approached the target area.

Scarcely 45 minutes after the last bomber of the Fifteenth had left
Regensburg/Prufening, the first of 102 Fortresses of the Eighth appeared
over the target to begin their bombing run. A total of 175 tons of high explosive and 79.7 tons of incendiaries were dropped in this mission, and the
already flailing aircraft plant received further damage. An interpretation of
photos taken the day following this double blow showed the almost complete destruction of the entire plant.

Other targets were now under attack. Air forces of 159 B-17's dropped a
heavy load of explosives and fragmentation bombs on the Messerschmitt
assembly plant at Regensburg/Obertraubling. The target was well covered,
and hits were scored on assembly shops, sub-assemblies, a boiler house, and
the landing ground. Of the ninety aircraft visible on the ground, it was
believed that at least twenty-five were destroyed. At the Messerschmitt factory at Augsburg, 199 B-17's dropped 369.5 tons of GP and 133.9 tons of
IE. Hangars, workshops, and research and administration buildings were
heavily damaged. The main target at Furth was the Messerschmitt component and assembly factory. After receiving 249.5 tons of GP, 59.5 tons IE,
and 110.3 tons fragmentation bombs, most of the target was in flames, and
of the 54 aircraft sighted on the field, 38 were probably damaged. The least
successful phase of these operations was the attack on the ball-bearing plant

at Stuttgart. Here fifty-two Flying Forts dropped most of their bombs west of the factory; only one burst fell in a corner of the target area.

Opposition to the Eighth's operations was less than expected. German attacks during the penetration were not aggressive, and became progressively milder on the withdrawal. Although thirty-one bombers were lost during the day's actions, this was not a high price to pay for the successful bombing of many targets, considering the number of planes involved. Bomber claims were 33-3-9, and fighter claims were 26-4-13. According to the Tactical Mission Report:

> "The simultaneous threat against southern Germany from two directions by the two forces of the U.S. Strategic Air Force appears to have caused the enemy controller to dissipate his forces to the extent that neither of the attacking forces could be successfully countered."

The combined operation of 25 February ended the six day offensive against the sources of German aircraft production and marked the virtual end of February's operations. (226 B-17's attempted to attack the Messerschmitt plant in Brunswick on 29 February, but owing to cloud, there was no observation of results.) One outstanding characteristic of this six-day period was the high degree of coordination between the Eighth and Fifteenth Air Forces and between the Eighth and the RAF. The heavy night attacks, which the British unleashed against Leipzig (19-20 February), Stuttgart (20-21 February), Schweinfurt (24-25 February), and Augsburg (25-26 February), were closely connected to the Eighth's operations; likewise, the Fifteenth, whenever weather permitted, tried to time its blows against southern Germany and Austria to coincide with the Eighth's assault in northern Europe. In the opinion of the USAAF historian, "This coordination, together with other counter-air force aspects of these operations, unquestionably held Allied bomber losses far below they might otherwise have been against these stoutly defended targets." Some idea of the scale of the effort involved can be gained from the following tables:

Operations 20-25 February 1944				
Heavy Bombers Dispatched:				
8th:	15th:	Total:	RAF:	Grand Total:
3,600	1,540	5,140	2,749	7,880
Heavy Bombers Attacking:				
8th:	15th:	Total:	RAF:	Grand Total:
3,116	800	3,916	2,300	6,218
Tonnage dropped:				
8th:	15th:	Total:	RAF:	Grand Total:
5,150	1,825	6,975	8,330	15,305

The damage inflicted on the German aircraft industry seems to have been great. Erla at Leipzig was one of the worst hit; according to CSS estimates, its pre-raid output of 250 Me-109s per month fell to 160 in February and nil in March. The complex at Regensburg was bombed by both strategic air forces and was heavily damaged. It was believed that its January output of 225 Me-109s could not be regained until August 1944; it was assumed that the Germans would prefer to disperse this factory rather than try to rebuild at the ruined site. The Ago aircraft plant at Oschersleben was not quite so heavily damaged by the attacks of 11 January, and 20 and 22 February. It was assumed that only a month's output was lost. The units of the Junkers complex at Halberstadt, Oschersleben, and Bernburg were believed to have been seriously hurt. The attacks on Halberstaut (wings) and Oschersleben (fuselages) probably complemented each others, although the results of the attacks on these "deep processes" could hardly be felt for a month or so.

CSS estimated that serious ancillary effects would result from the fact that many of these blows were simultaneous. Some of the factories lost stocks of tools and jig-making machinery, which could have serious effects since outside jig makers were undoubtedly swamped with orders, The scheduled transfer of Gothaer to the production of the FW-190 might have started by the time of the big raid on Gotha. If this were so, the heavy destruction at Gotha might have wiped out a large supply of FW-190 jigs, which would indirectly affect other factories. Finally, the causalities, which were probably heavy, could be expected to slow down production by causing a shortage of skilled labor.

Air Ministry estimates tended to support the optimistic interpretation of the CCS. March estimates for the production of the Me-109 were 225 as compared to 400 estimated for February; these figures included salvaged as well as new output. However, the FW-190 factories, which were less severely damaged in the Big Week attacks, managed to increase production from 200 in February to 275 in March - both figures including salvaged planes.

Information obtained from high-ranking officers in the Wehrmacht and Luftwaffe after the collapse of Germany testifies to the effectiveness of the February attacks. In the opinion of Generalleutnant Adolf Galland, Commanding General of the Fighter Forces and one of the most famous fighter pilots of the German Air Force with 104 aerial victories, the attacks by our strategic bombers early in 1944 "practically destroyed German fighter production for a short period." Of particular significance is the evidence contributed by Dr. Karl Frydag, head of aircraft production for the German Air Force, while being interrogated by American intelligence officers:

Q: Would you say roughly that as a direct result of the February 1944 attacks approximately four thousand aircraft were lost to the German Air Force? Your statement was 50% of the production was lost for two and a half months.

A: Yes, that is right. Only an exceptional effort could come up to that figure and thatwas an effort we could not have kept up.

Operations for the month as a whole were the largest yet undertaken in air war. The Eight Air Force put 7,190 bombers over target for a loss of only 3.8 percent of the attacking force. Bomb tonnage was 19,146 and bomber and fighter claims of destroyed enemy aircraft amounted to 740 planes.

Weather and enemy action hampered the Fifteenth Air Force. Some 2,300 effective bomber sorties were carried out, with losses at 5.4 percent. The bomb load came to 8,747 tons, and 355 enemy aircraft were claimed destroyed.

The Eights participation in the operations of 20-25 February can be shown in the following tables:

Date	Dispatched	Lost	Claims
Feb 20	1,003	21	65-33-29
Feb 21	861	16	19-16-14
Feb 22	467	41	34-18-17
Feb 24	809	49	83-22-42
Feb 25	754	31	49-11-26

As the Big Week ended, General Arnold cabled his congratulations to the Commanding General of the U.S. Strategic Air Forces, stating his attacks on Regensburg, Leipzig, Gotha, Bernburg, and other vital fighter factories were wiping out German fighter production. He expressed his thanks to all ranks in the command from top to bottom for the superb job they were doing and wished them all the best in continuing to carry destruction through the heart of Germany.

6

OPERATIONS DURING THE SPRING OF 1944

The period from the end of the Big Week to D-Day constitutes a definite phase in the war against the Luftwaffe and its supporting industries. It is characterized by certain changes of policy, not only of the attacking forces but also on the part of the Germans. During the first large-scale attacks in the fall of 1943, the Germans often tried to rebuild their plants at the original sites; where this was not practical, they tried to spread the resources, originally planned for expansion, into dispersal factories. As the attacks increased in weight and number, the process of dispersal was greatly accelerated, and it is quite possible that this, in addition to the air offensive, helped to keep down production during the last three months of 1943. However, the Germans were gambling for survival and could afford to forgo a temporary advantage if it would profit them in the long run. The decision to disperse undoubtedly saved aircraft production; thus the GAF, although terribly crippled, was able to survive the attacks of 20-25 February.

During the three months that elapsed between the end of Operation ARGUMENT, the formal name for the raids of the Big Week, and the immediate preparation for D-Day, German aircraft factories were distributed out of the great complexes and into new centers, some of which were underground. The Italian aircraft industry was brought more closely under

German control, and tools and machinery were sent from the Reich to improve production methods. On 21 February, the monthly production of Italian aircraft was estimated as follows:

Fighters:	107
Trainers:	30
Bomber Transports	35

Italian production of aero-engines was estimated at 150 per month, and it was believed that some of the Daimler-Benz machinery had been shipped to Italy.

Meanwhile, additional Me-109 output was being developed at Brasov, Rumania, and Gyor, Hungary. The Hungarian Car and Machinery Works in Gyor had been manufacturing a wide variety of war equipment since 1941. According to ground intelligence, plans for 1944 production called for a monthly output of 50 Me-109's; it was believed that the Germans were sending production machinery to Gyor to avoid the bombing further west.

These new developments in German aircraft production were largely within the Fifteenth's sphere of operation. With its principal POINT-BLANK effort directed against Messerschmitt production, it had attacked the Weiner Neustadt complex on 2 November and stopped work there for several months. By the end of March, the Fifteenth was ready to turn its attention to the second unit of the complex, the Machinery Werke aircraft factory in the Vienna area, and to the new production centers at Gyor and Brasov. In addition, attacks were planned for other vitals of the complex now dispersed to plants in Austria and Yugoslavia, including a network of smaller plants in the Vienna area. As February ended, a new target priority was received at Fifteenth Air Force headquarters; accordingly, the following priorities were set up:

1. Szigetszentmiklos, Hungry (ball-bearings)
2. Stuttgart (ball-bearings)
3. Fischen, Germany (Me-109)
4. Budapest (Me-109)
5. Schwechat, Austria (Me-209)

6. Friedrichshafen, Germany (Do-217)
7. Friedrichshafen, other plants
8. Frankfurt (Me-109)

Additional information on the eastward dispersal of the GAF was soon forthcoming. Photo reconnaissance of the Budapest/Weiss airfield revealed an assembly plant that seemed to be engaged in the final assembly of the Me-410, possibly in connection with the plant Szigetszentmiklos (Hungary). The Macchi aircraft plant at Varese, Italy, was now confirmed as an active producer of the single seat MC-205 fighter, with monthly output estimates at 50 aircraft. Since the Big Week, the Italian aircraft industry had increased in importance, and it was believed that the Luftwaffe would have to use some Italian fighters to make up for their losses. On 5 March, General Eaker informed the commander of the Fifteenth, General Twining, that photo reconnaissance indicated large concentrations of enemy aircraft at six German fields including Oberpfaffenhofen and Poker. These fields were to be hit whenever the opportunity offered, but such problems should not be allowed to interfere with primary objectives.

Unfortunately, the incredibly bad weather, which had hampered the operations of the Fifteenth Air Force ever since its activation, persisted throughout much of the spring of 1944. Although the weather in northern Italy was not too bad, there were few POINTBLANK targets in this area. Storms in the trans-Alpine region frequently prevented the deep penetrations that the more important POINTBLANK objectives required. Consequently, the Fifteenth devoted most of its operations during March to the support of the land battle in Italy, especially the Anzio and Monte Cassino actions.

In England, the Eighth Air Force continued its attacks on prescribed strategic targets, assisted by the Ninth. (Ninth Air Force missions, which were only partly devoted to POINTBLANK are not treated here.) There was no fundamental change in the priorities, and the Luftwaffe and its sources of supply still remained a chief objective. Weather was often the factor that determined the sequences and number of attacks delivered against a particular target.

By this time the impressive build-up of theater strength – there were approximately 1,156 heavy bombers operational with units – permitted the Eighth to afford heavy air battles, and it was the deliberate policy of headquarters to entice the German formations into the air by all possible means. According to General Spaatz, three of the March attacks were flown without any attempt at deception, the route followed in each attack being the same. General Doolittle succinctly characterized the situation: "It is now a case of either the Hun will fold or we will fold." The odds, however, were in favor of the Eighth.

In theory, USSTAF felt it desirable to relax its pressure against the bases and facilities of the Luftwaffe in order to pay greater attention to high-priority industrial targets. Since the great increase of theater strength and the development of the long-range fighter practically assured its air superiority, it would be possible to keep the German fighter force "in a state of relative impotency rather than complete destruction." However this idea remained largely theoretical during March, for the weather often arbitrarily forced attacks on western airfields by covering everything farther inland with a deep overcast.

The Eighth's first counter-air force operation of the month occurred on 2 March. While a heavy force was sent to Frankfurt, 106 bombers attacked the airfield at the famous old cathedral city of Chartres, France. Some 150 tons of explosives were dropped without any opposition; the ground haze coming up from the fields made timing difficult, and the strike photos indicated only fair results.

Airfields were also the target for the Fifteenth. On the 3nd of March, small forces bombed Viterbo, Canino, and Fabrica di Roma without conspicuous success. The Eighth returned to the attack on 5 March by scheduling missions against German-held airdromes in France. Unfortunately, 10/10 cloud covered all the primary targets, and the 219 Liberators were forced to bomb Cognac, Bergerac, and Landes de Bussac through holes in the overcast. The results varied; though they were believed to be good at Cognac and Bergerac, they were very ineffective at Landes de Bussac. Four bombers were destroyed and claims of 14-0-12 were made.

In spite of the heavy blows delivered against it in February, the Luftwaffe was still capable of a fierce defense of targets considered vital. This was clearly shown by the great air battle of 6 March. On this day, 740 heavy bombers were dispatched by the Eighth against Berlin. In spite of the fact that the bombers were escorted by 796 fighters of the VIII and IX Fighter Commands and two squadrons of RAF Mustangs, the opposition was unusually heavy. Approximately 615 German fighters rose to defend the Reich, making this the largest defensive effort yet carried out by the GAF. In addition to the usual single-engine fighters, twin-engine and single-engine night fighters were called into the battle. As the formations reached the Hanover area, the 3d Division was subjected to intense attack. The bombers of this division formed a line of combat wing pairs approximately sixty miles long with the escort fighters slightly weaker in the middle than at the two ends. Taking advantage of this, the German fighter controller attacked the front and the rear of the formation with forces of moderate size. While the escorts were occupied with this attack, he threw more than 100 fighters at the momentarily unprotected center. This maneuver proved to be most effective; in about thirty minutes, the German fighters had destroyed some twenty bombers. When the bombers passed north of Brunswick, the attacks from this first line of defense ceased, but when the 1st Division reached the Berlin area, the air battle began again, continuing until the bombers left the area.

Some of the fighter escorts were subjected to attack as the formations crossed into Germany, but the majority of the Geschwader concentrated their strikes against the low bomber groups. (Geschwaders means a tactical air wing; each had between 90 to 120 aircraft.) Some of the formations were under fire for as long as two hours and forty-five minutes, and the Germans tried all types of tactics. Rocket attacks and air-to-air bombing were attempted, and a new type of projectile (believed to be a fuzed 20-mm. incendiary shell), which burst with a sparkling effect and invariably set fire to aircraft which it hit, was seen for the first time. Anti-aircraft fire over the Berlin area was intense and accurate. Weather conditions at the target were unfavorable and the bombing was generally regarded as poor. A total of sixty-nine bombers and eleven fighters was the cost the AAF had to pay; however, the losses were not all on one side. The bombers claimed 93-44-66 German fighters, and the escort fighters listed 82-9-32 as destroyed, probably destroyed, and damaged.

On the 7th, the Fifteenth returned to the airfields in the Rome area, striking Fabrica di Roma, Orvieto, and two fields at Viterbo. Only at Fabrica di Roma and the main Viterbo field was assessment possible, with bursts showing on both those landing grounds. Clearing weather over northern Europe permitted the Eighth to make another attempt at the Berlin area on the 8th, and 620 bombers dropped 940.5 tons on the ball-bearing plant targeted. The excellent visibility permitted accurate bombing, and General Spaatz believed the target had been completely destroyed. Once again the Luftwaffe put up a sturdy defense as the loss of thiryt-seven bombers and seventeen fighters indicated. Total bomber and fighter claims came to 123-26-41.

After this there was a pause in the Eighth's POINTBLANK operations. Several missions were directed against robot-bomb installations in the Pas de Calais sector and there were the usual weather delays. On the 15th, 344 bombers were dispatched to bomb Brunswick, a city rich in aircraft targets. Unfortunately, when the planes reached their objective, they found it covered by 10/10 cloud; although 745 tons were dropped by means of blind-bombing equipment, the results were not observed. A dive-bombing mission accompanied by a low-level fighter sweep was carried out by 160 Mustangs on the 17th. On the following day, when a heavy force of bombers attempted to get through to strike airdromes and aircraft factories in south central Germany, the overcast again protected the primaries. The cities of Munich and Friedrichshafen, and five smaller targets of opportunity, were bombed instead.

As so often happened when the primaries were overcast and targets of opportunity were bombed, arrangements with the fighter escort were thoroughly upset. Many bombers missed the rendezvous with the fighters altogether; consequently, they were exceedingly vulnerable to the GAF attacks. Forty-three heavy bombers were lost of which four were destroyed in mid-air collisions, and one was struck by bombs from a friendly craft above it. The returning bombers made claims of 45-10-17; 15 fighters were lost and escort claims were 40-6-9.

While the Eighth was engaged in the skies over southern Germany, the Fifteenth was carrying out one of the most brilliantly planned aerial maneuvers of the European war. The target was a group of airfields and landing grounds located in the area surrounding Udine at the northern tip of the Adriatic. This "pocket of enemy air power," as a tactical mission report described it, operated directly against the most convenient routes from Italy to targets in Austria and southern Germany. It was a constant source of irritation to the Fifteenth Air Force. Recognizing the strategic importance of these bases, the Luftwaffe began to concentrate considerable strength on them early in 1944. The photo reconnaissance of 29 January showed approximately 170 fighters present in the area. The highly successful raids of 30 January reduced this number to about 70 undamaged planes; however, due to the important part these airfields played in the defense of southern Germany, the destroyed and damaged planes were replaced and fighter strength was gradually built up again. Recent photos of the fighter airfields at Lavariano, Maniago, Gorizia, Udine and Ossoppo, Italy, showed a total of 235 enemy aircraft, and it was known that the Villaorba landing ground was the main base for the German bombers harassing allied shipping in and around Anzio-Bettuno area. (When this photo reconnaissance was conducted, the Maniago field actually showed a drop from fifty to twenty aircraft present. However, at this time a raid was going on in the Vienna area, and it was assumed that some of the Maniago planes were taking part in the battle.)

To neutralize these fields and destroy the maximum number of enemy planes, a series of carefully planned and timed operations was worked out, and was mounted on the morning of 18 March. The first phase occurred when 95 P-38's took off at 0720 hours, rendezvoused at 1,000 San Severo, then flew off down the Adriatic at approximately 75 feet above the water to avoid radar detection. Nearing the coast, they rose to 6,000 feet and separated to perform their parts in the developing action. One group circled over Treviso, strafed trains and airfields, made a short patrol north to the mountains, and then flew to Venice to continue its nuisance activities. Others carried out a fighter sweep in great force at 0920 in the Udine/Villaorba area and succeeded in holding most of the enemy fighters on the ground.

Meanwhile, 113 B-17's had been flying up the Yugoslav coast making a feint toward southern Germany and flushing up the fighters based in the Klagenfurt and Graz areas. When the bombers reached a point northeast of

Fiume, instead of continuing into southern Germany, they turned sharply west drawing the Klagenfurt/Graz attacking forces with them. Shortly afterwards, at 1013 hours they dropped 20 lb. fragmentation bombs on the Villaorba and Udine landing grounds. Just as the bombing ceased, the Klagenfurt/Graz fighters, who had considerably extended themselves, had to land to refuel; however, because of the damage to the fields just bombed, they had to come down at other near-by bases.

The stage was thus set for the final phase. While the enemy aircraft normally based in the area were concentrated on the ground, together with the fighters from the Klagenfurt and Graz areas, three task forces of 72, 67, and 121 Liberators swept in to blast the fields at Gorizia, Lavariano, and Maniago between 1059 and 1111 hours. The effect was devastating: a total of 32,370, 20 lb. fragmentation bombs dropped; only two enemy aircraft were able to get off the ground to intercept the B-24 forces. This raid was a heavy blow to enemy air power in northern Italy. In the official report, the task forces were credited with destroying or damaging fifyt-eight aircraft on the ground. Bomber claims for the aerial battle were 23-7-9, and the fighters claimed 33-3-3. Losses were extremely light: of the 498 bombers and 176 fighters that went out, 7 and 4, respectively, failed to return.

The next day, the Fifteenth launched a follow-up blow at Klagenfurt and Graz. The Klagenfurt airdrome was hit by 234 heavy bombers that dropped 565.65 tons of HE and incendiary bombs early in the afternoon. Smoke made it difficult to assess the damage, but hits were seen on hangars, administration buildings, dispersal areas, and the landing field. Thirty-two fighters and seven bomber-transports were seen on the field: thirteen of the former and three of the latter were claimed destroyed. Between forty and fifty enemy aircraft attacked the bombers in waves, shooting down two bombers, while two more were lost to flak and another two collided. Graz was attacked by 76 aircraft dropping 100.2 tons of 500 lb. and 63.1 tons of 100 lb. bombs. Photos showed the bombs falling in the southwest part of the city. Fifteen enemy planes were destroyed and twelve Liberators were lost. The same day 74 P-47's and P-51's of the Eighth Air Force made a combination dive-bombing attack and fighter sweep on the Gilze-Rijen (Dutch) airdromes and surrounding country. Some hits were reported on the northwest portion of the field and near ammunition stores, but in general the bombing was only fair. There was neither any opposition nor reported claims or losses.

A big operation was planned for 23 March when the Eighth assigned some 750 heavy bombers to attack aircraft factories and airdromes in western and central Germany. However, cloud conditions interfered with bombing, and dense and persistent contrails made it hard to keep the formations together. Only some eighty planes were able to get through to the assigned primaries. A total of 1,755 tons were dropped including tonnage dropped on some additional targets of opportunity. A change in the wind caused considerable confusion as the lead group reached the IP forty-three minutes ahead of time, and other formations were twenty to twenty-five minutes early. This naturally made it difficult for the escorts to locate the bomber formations and the Brunswick force was completely unescorted. The results of the bombing were difficult to estimate. The airfield received a good many bursts on and around its installations, and one targeted factory at Brunswick may have been hit, but cloud cover prevented a successful photo reconnaissance. Enemy attacks were aggressive, with twenty-seven bombers failing to return.

Weather again interfered with the mission of 24 March. A force of some 200 B-17's was sent to bomb the ball-bearing plant at Schweinfurt while another group of more than 200 B-24's were to strike at airfields in northwestern France. Heavy clouds covered the targets for the most part, and dense contrails prevailed; only one formation of fifty-five forts attacked Schweinfurt with radar equipment, and the results were questionable. The airfields received 403.7 tons from the B-24s dropped at medium altitude with excellent results. The enemy provided practically no opposition to this mission.

A more extensive counter-airdrome operation was carried out on the 27th. Clouds covered central Europe but in the west the weather was clear. Consequently a large force of 707 bombers was sent out to attack eight fighter airdromes and one factory in west and northwest France. The targets were significant in that they were fields used for pilot training, two reserve training units (Chartres and Tours, France), recce (reconnaissance), FW-190 repairs (Tours, France) and one fighter base.

All bombing was done visually and 980 tons were dropped. With the exception of the Tours repair depot, all the objectives were well covered, and the bombing was considered good. The next day a force of 373 B-17's and 77 B-24's were sent to attack airfields in France again. Because of deteriorating weather conditions, the Liberators were all recalled before reaching the targets; however, the Fortresses pressed on, dropping 936.5 tons of bombs. The results at Chartres and Dijon were good and only fair at Reims and Chateaudun. The accompanying fighters claimed 30-1-33 for aircraft attacked on the ground. Losses were light: two bombers and three fighters.

#

These operations virtually ended the counter-air operations for March both in England and in Italy. On the whole, it was a month marked by much greater activity against airfields than against the basic factories of the aircraft industry. In the case of the Eighth Air Force, weather prevented a heavier effort against the industry, for POINTBLANK was still the number one commitment. The Eighth dropped a total of 21,348 tons during the month in 8,596 effective sorties for losses of 4.1 percent of the attacking forces. A very large number of German fighters were claimed destroyed during the month, the total being no fewer than 834 planes of which 363 were credited to the bombers.

The Fifteenth Air Force was equally handicapped by some of the worst weather observed in years; however, unlike the Eighth, it was also involved in occasional support of ground battle. A certain amount of time and effort were spent on the Anzio operations, on the Cassino battle, and in attacks on rail communications in the peninsula. Theoretically, POINTBLANK remained the top priority for the Fifteenth, but for the aforementioned reasons, little could be done against the aircraft factories located across the Alps in Austria and southern Germany. Instead, counter-air operations took the form of attacks against airdromes. This not only satisfied General Arnold's instructions to hit the Luftwaffe in the air and on the ground but also gave support to the ground battle. A total of 1,731 tons was dropped on these targets during the month, as compared with 417 tons dropped on similar objectives in February; however, the March tonnage on aircraft and components factories was 894 tons. Losses were considerably less than in the previous month, being only 2 percent of the 4,201 effective sorties. Joint bomber and fighter claims of destroyed enemy aircraft came to 210.

Naturally the many demands on the Fifteenth Air Force sometimes produced disagreements in the high places. Something like this took place toward the end of March. General Sir Henry Maitland Wilson, the theater commander, had ordered the strategic force to proceed against the marshalling yards at Bucharest, Ploesti, and other Italian targets, although Air Marshal Sir Charles Portal had decided that Ploesti was not to be bombed. General Spaatz requested General Arnold to straighten the matter with the higher authorities, stating that it seemed there were too many people giving orders to the Fifteenth, and that he could not accept responsibility for the control of the strategic force until the matter was clarified.

This cable produced some deliberation and action. General Arnold at once protested to Air Marshal Portal against the diversion of the Fifteenth into Balkan operations. It was his understanding that General Spaatz should control the strategic air forces under Portal's direction, as provided for by the Combined Chiefs of Staff. At the same time, General Anderson and General Charles P. Cabell, director of plans for the USSTAF protested against the apparent desire of the British to give the theater commanders the right to direct strategic attacks against political objectives – for example, the desire to attack partisans in the Balkans– whenever desired.

In his reply to Arnold, Portal stated that he respected the command arrangements made and did not wish to deviate from them, but the British believed a very favorable situation existed in the Balkans, and he wished to exploit it. He urged the theater commander in the Mediterranean be given authority to order the Fifteenth to attack certain Balkan targets. The matter came before CCS almost immediately and their decision was in favor of the British request. Arnold continued to insist, however, that Balkan's targets should be attacked only when weather prevented attacks against primary objectives. He concluded by requesting Portal assure him "the advantages and disadvantages of all diversions from the main effort are carefully weighed by you."

Following the decision of CCS, a new order of priority for the Fifteenth Air Force was set up. First place was given to the requirements of the battle of Italy, second went to POINTBLANK and third was given to targets in southeastern Europe. It was also stated that when the occasion warranted, General Wilson and General Spaatz could deviate from the established priorities to attack other targets of current political and military importance. The ban on attacking targets in Hungary was abolished.

After these basic policies had been formulated, detailed operational instructions were received at Fifteenth Air Force headquarters on 29 March. Ten major targets were listed in the following priority:

1. Steyr-Daimler-Puch factory and ball-bearing plant, Steyr, Austria
2. Fischamend, Austria, first unit of the Me-109 complex at Wiener Neustadt
3. Wiener Neustadt Werke I
4. Bad Voslau, Austria factory and airdrome
5. Duna aircraft plant,Me-210 and me-410, Szigetszentmiklos, Hungary and the Budapest/Tokol factory and airdrome, Hungry
6. Hungarian Wagon and machine works, Gyor, Hungary
7. The aircraft factory at Brasov, Rumania
8. Messerschmitt factory at Augsburg
9. Oberplaffenhofen factory near Munich, Germany
10. Schwechat factory, Austria

Aalthough in second place, the Fischamend plant was believed to be the largest remaining unit of the Wiener Neustadt Messerschmitt complex, and was probably producing wings and other Me-109 components. Werk I at Wiener Neustadt was reviving and was presumably assembling at least 75 Me-109's per month. It was linked with the Bad Voslau plant. The Dana and the Tokol factories were supposed to be assembling both Me-210's and -410's. The facilities at Brasov, Augsburg, and Oberpfaffenhofen were involved in the production of the Me-410, while the Schwechat plant was supposed to be making a few jets and possibly assembling the Me-219 night fighter.

In case weather prevented attacks on the primary targets, secondaries were listed as follows:

1. Macchi aircraft factory at Varese, Italy
2. Fiat factory and airfield at Turin
3. Breda gun works at the Bresso/Milan airfield
4. The extension of the Wiener Neustadt complex at Klagenfurt, Austria, and
5. Its extension at Zemun, Yugoslavia, where the Ikarus and Rogerzarski factory was producing and repairing Me-109's
6. Muller ball-bearing factory at Nuremberg

On 3 April a few modifications were made in both lists. The Bad Voslau factory was moved up to third place in the primaries, and in the secondaries, the Fiat plant became first priority, Klagenfurt was put in third rank and Breda was dropped.

The emphasis on relatively new targets in these directives is indicative of the progress of dispersal in the German aircraft industry. Since many of these plants were in central or southeastern Europe, they affected the operational policies of the Fifteenth more than those of the Eighth. Some new plants and some expanded old ones were bombed, but it was not considered possible to locate and destroy all of them. Rather, it was decided to pound the ball-bearing industry hard, and try to concentrate on a small number of large aero-engine component and assembly plants. This, plus the strategy of attacking finished enemy planes on the ground wherever they could be found, was considered the best way to hold down the Luftwaffe if it could not be totally destroyed.

Both the Eighth and the Fifteenth were faced with priority conflicts during the spring of 1944. In England there was a tendency for the strategic effort to swing to the bombardment of tactical targets in preparation for OVERLORD, the invasion of Europe, and in Italy a great deal of emphasis was placed on the destruction of rail facilities, as a result of the insistence of Air Marshal Tedder. Nonetheless, the pressure on the GAF was kept up as much as possible.

In keeping with the new directive, the Fifteenth launched an attack on the Steyr ball-bearing plant, the number one priority, on 2 April. The

German ball-bearing industry had been a frequent target for attacks by both strategic air forces. After the heavy raids on Schweinfurt, the Steyrwaffen Walzlagerwerk had become one of the most important ball-bearing plants in the Reich. Once an aero-engine works, it was now known to be producing bearings and ball-bearing assemblies for the German Government. Although this plant had been heavily damaged by the Fifteenth in previous raids, the latest reconnaissance showed definite signs of activity. A recent photo coverage of the Wiener Neustadt complex revealed that its capacity for aircraft assembly was being increased and it was thought that the Steyr plant might, in some way, be connected with this. For this reason it was decided to strike it in force.

At noon on the 2d, 127 B-17's and 137 B-24's, escorted by Lightnings and Thunderbolts on penetration and 78 Lightning's for target cover and withdrawal, roared over the Steyr plant at altitudes from 19,000 to 25,000 feet. Nearly 700 tons of bombs were dropped with great success. In two ball-bearing and two cage-manufacturing buildings the damage was practically total, and in the packing and dispatching building, fifty percent of the roofing collapsed. The testing and assembly building received one direct hit and the receiving depot got two direct hits and two near misses. At the same time, a force of 168 B-24's bombed the Steyr airfield with 333.80 tons, yet failed to do any damage to the main structures. A freshman force of 28 B-24's attacked an airdrome as a secondary target.

The attack on the Steyr plant produced a sharp reaction from the Luftwaffe. The bomber crews estimated that they were attacked by 250 to 300 enemy planes, and believed they had shot down 84. The majority of the intercepting fighters were from the Vienna-Graz- Klagenfurt area, with the exception of sixty or seventy aircraft from fields east of Fiume, a former Free State, and a few from Munich. As a result of this mission, Steyr ball-bearing plant was suspended from the priorities list; pending more definite information, the undamaged portions of the Steyr-Daimler-Puch factory were classified as "secondary target(s) of low priority."

The next three operations of the Fifteenth against POINTBLANK targets were on a smaller scale. On 3 April a force of 112 Fortresses bombed the Budapest/Tokol aircraft factory with 331.75 tons. Although enemy attacks were aggressive, only four bombers failed to return. Strike photos

showed 350 craters within the precincts of the factory, but only two buildings received serious damage. On the night of 3-4 April 7, Liberators and 70
Wellingtons dropped high explosives and incendiaries on the Manfred
Weiss works at Budapest. A good concentration of bombing was reported
with two large explosions and many fires. On the 6th, a force of 97 bombers
was sent to the Zagreb, Yugoslavia airdrome; however, only 19 Liberators
were able to attack due to a heavy overcast. No bombing results could be
observed.

After an absence of 10 days, the Eighth Air Force began a period of
intense POINTBLANK activity by staging an operation against several targets in northwest Germany on the 8th. Nine combat wings were committed; 314 B-17's were to attack five Luftwaffe installations, and 330 B-24's
were to bomb two aircraft factories in Brunswick. Although the Forts
encountered no opposition, the Liberators which spearheaded the attack
ran into considerable air battle. At first, nothing happened as the bombers
passed Lingen, then Dummer Lake, Steinhuder Lake, Hanover, and even
Brunswick without seeing any sign of the enemy. About 40 miles northeast
of Brunswick the formations ran into a concentration of 150 enemy fighters.
A fierce combat resulted where the 2nd Division lost thirty planes, although
it appears that the American fighter escorts outnumbered the attacking
planes. The heavy bomber losses can be partly explained by a navigational
error made by one of the combat wings of the 2nd Division. This wing
turned south too soon and flew an "inside course" to Brunswick, placing
itself some sixty miles ahead of the scheduled escort pattern. In the words of
an official report, this wing "suffered the usual consequences of such a navigational error. The enemy exploited the situation with his usual alacrity and
effectiveness."

The bombing of the Me-110 plant in the Wilhelmitor suburb of Brunswick produced excellent results. The 362 tons of bombs were well distributed, with every building in the installation hit. Owing to navigational difficulties, many of the B-17's were unable to reach their assigned objectives;
many targets of opportunity had to be sought. As a result, the following
GAF airfields were attacked with generally good results: Langenhagen (142
tons), Hesslingen (152.5 tons), Oldenburg (147 tons), Hesepe (39.6 tons),
Twente Enschede (41.8 tons), Handorf (36 tons), Achner (112.5 tons),

and Rheine (41 tons). The VIII Bomber Command lost thirty-four planes in this operation and twenty-two fighters were missing also. Total bomber and fighter claims against the enemy were 148-25-58.

Another extensive operation was planned for the next day, 9 April. This was to be a very deep penetration of the Reich to attack Focke-Wulf factories in north central Germany and Poland. A total of 542 bombers were airborne, but high clouds over England hindered the formation assembly: only 402 planes actually reached the targets. The German opposition was vigorous in some areas, but in general it was sporadic and confused. The enemy seemed uncertain both as to the destination and the withdrawal route of the bombers; the heaviest attacks finally fell on a portion of the returning bombers who chose to fly a course farther south than planned. Had they kept to the briefed route, they would have probably missed the German interceptors who were nearly out of fuel. By returning some ninety miles farther south than intended, they flew into a concentration of some sixty single-and twin-engine fighters, with some bombers lost.

The Focke-Wulf plant at Marienburg was well bombed with 217.5 tons dropped from medium altitude. Various assembly shops received direct hits, and twenty-five percent of one subassembly building was destroyed. Office buildings were damaged and fires started in the barracks. At Gydnia/Rahmel, Poland the bombing was done by a relatively small force and was considered fair to good. Warnemünde, Germany, and its aircraft installations received severe injuries; a heavy concentration landed on the north end of the workshop area and there was another good pattern on the marshalling yards and the warehouse area. A small force attacked the FW airframe factory at Posen scoring many hits, while another small formation attacked Rostock with poor results. At Tutow 106 Liberators dropped 270.8 tons with fair results. There was a concentration on the aircraft installations between the two airfields and photos showed many fires burning. On the various phases of this operation, a total of 31 bombers and 10 fighters were lost; combined, fighter and bomber claims came to 63-15-30.

On 10 April another blow was delivered against the dwindling reserve strength of the Luftwaffe. A force of 486 B-17's and 243 B-24's was dispatched to attack air bases and centers of production and repair in Belgium and France. In coordination with the main operation, one combat wing of

Liberators attacked a military installation in the Pas de Calais area while two groups of P-38 fighter-bombers attacked two French airdromes. Weather interfered with attacks on four primaries, but all other objectives were hit. The attacks on the aircraft repair centers at Brussels and Bourges, France, were particularly successful. Eight airdromes and fields were bombed and the enemy opposition was very weak, suggesting the Luftwaffe was not prepared to commit itself in force to the defense of northwest Europe.

The favorable weather conditions, which permitted these operation,s may have influenced General Spaatz to schedule a modified form of operation ARGUMENT which had been so successfully carried out during 20-25 February. At any rate, on 11 April he signaled Eaker via the Redline communication system that the weather looked very favorable for combined operations, and he wished the Fifteenth to attack Wiener Neustadt, Fischamend, and Bad Voslau while the Eighth attacked Schweinfurt, Tutow, Zwickau, Leipzig, and Halle. However, for reasons which are unclear, the plan was abandoned after several postponements.

Meanwhile, the Eighth continued its large-scale assault on the aircraft industry deep   within the Reich. The emphasis continued to be placed on the Focke-Wulf plants, in   comparison with earlier efforts which had been directed largely against the Messerschmitt complexes. On the 11th, a big mission was planned against six FW-190 and Junkers assembly plants far in the interior of Germany. The tactics were strongly reminiscent of the very successful operation of 20 February. The main force composed of the 2d Division was to proceed along the well-traveled Zuider Zee-Hanover-Berlin route to Oschersleben and Bernburg, and was to be followed by the lst Division en route to Cottbus and Sorau, Germany. At the same time, an unescorted diversionary force made up of the 3rd Division was to proceed over the North Sea to Rosen.

Unfortunately, the Germans seem to have solved this particular form of attack. The Rosen force's course was accurately predicted from the outset; it was intercepted over the Baltic Sea by a force of twin- and single-engine fighters which flew directly from the Berlin area. Heavy attacks followed; as the weather was deteriorating, the attack on Rosen was abandoned and alternates including Rostock were bombed instead. Here again, the resistance was strong, and as a result of its lack of fighter protection the 3rd Division lost 33 bombers.

Meanwhile the 2nd and 1st Divisions, to list them in their order of flight, were apparently neglected by the Luftwaffe, and penetrated the air over Hanover before they were attacked. Then about 150 enemy aircraft concentrated in the Hanover-Brunswick-Bernburg area launched heavy attacks on the American formation, the 1st Division being severely harassed and sustaining considerable losses.

At Bernburg, the Ju-88 and -188 Assembly factory received 289.3 tons of GP and fragmentation bombs as well as 57.2 tons of incendiaries. Three large bursts covered the main assembly shop and there were isolated hits on offices, hangars, and barracks. The FW-190 assembly at Oschersleben was visited by 181 B-24's dropping explosives and incendiaries with good results. Sorau, Germany, which contained another FW-190 assembly, was bombed for the first time by the Eighth Air Force. The target area was covered by six large concentrations, and there were direct hits on important installations. Damage to the town itself was severe. A small force of 35 B-17's dropped 7 tons on an aero-engine factory at Arnswalde, now part of Poland, placing direct hits on the corner of a large assembly area and 9 direct hits on another shop. Politz, Gulzow, and four other area in Germany were hit. Of the 817 bombers dispatched, 64 were lost, making this operation one of the more costly days of the war. The German losses, according to the claims of the bombers and fighters, were 124 destroyed, 24 probable's, and 33 damaged. As General Clayton Lawrence Bissell, Assistant Chief of Staff for G-2 stated: "Determined German air resistance in defense of vital targets [in] Germany proper [is] still being encountered." Air superiority seemed elusive that day.

#

Weather prevented a big mission for the 12th, but the skies cleared the following day, April 13, 1944, and big mission was possible. The targets were the German twin-engine fighter centers at Augsburg, Lechfeld, and Oberpfaffenhofen, and the ball-bearing factory at Schweinfurt which had been partially repaired since the last attack by the VIII Bomber Command. The weather was clear and the operation was flown essentially as planned, with the 1st Division leading two others until the Moselle River in Germany was reached; here the 1st continued onto Schweinfurt and the other two turned south to Augsburg and the other objectives. The 1st Division received almost the entire enemy attack.

The German fighters assembled in the Juvincourt-Reims area in France well to the south of the formations, out of range of any American escorts roving ahead of the bombers. After assembly they proceeded north, receiving reinforcements from bases in Belgium and the southern Netherlands. By this time the enemy fighters were over 160 strong; with this formidable concentration, they engaged the bombers of the 1st Division just north of Trier. At this time, the entire fighter escort of the division consisted of 43 P-47's. As this fierce combat broke up, the formations came into the Frankfurt area where another 100 single-engine fighters were assembling; some of the fighters had flown 220 miles from remote bases to take part in the engagement, and when the battle was joined they threw themselves enthusiastically into the melee. The small force of P-47s was inadequate to defend the formations; in spite of their best efforts, 11 bombers went down to the enemy fighter assaults. By this time the target area was reached and the bombs were dropped; shortly afterwards, a force of Mustangs which had gone on ahead to clear twenty fighters from the Wertheim area rejoined the Thunderbolts, and the enemy fighters retired. From this point back to England, the 1st Division was unopposed. Nor were the other two task forces seriously engaged by the enemy. Either he had concentrated all his efforts on the 1st Division, or a raid by the Fifteenth (see below) in the Budapest area had drawn the Luftwaffe away from southern Germany.

The bombing was, on the whole, successful. Schweinfurt was struck by 343 tons, which covered most of the targeted plant. Photos showed that the entire west art of Werk I was severely damaged. At Werk II, three direct hits on a large assembly and machine shop were seen, although smoke and debris made observation difficult. The Lechfeld airdrome, believed to be a testing field for Me-410's and experimental aircraft of the Messerschmitt plant at Augsburg, received 248.0 Tons of GP and IB with results that were believed to be good. Oberpfaffenhofen, an important factory and airfield for the Dornier Do-217, and possibly for the Me-410, was bombed by 60 Liberators with fair results. The heaviest bomb load fell on the aircraft factory at Augsburg where 207 B-17's dropped 424 tons. Hits were seen on subassembly machine shops, a power house and a flight hangar. There were incendiary strikes on two round hangars and machine and press shops. The great volume of smoke made further assessment impossible. The cost of this operation was thirty-eight bombers, with total claims against the enemy at 124-26-59.

While the Eighth was carrying out these intensive actions against the German aircraft industry, farther south the Fifteenth was making its contribution to the same end. On 9 April a modification of Operational Instruction No. 18 was sent to the Fifteenth. This new order included the Repulogepyar aircraft plant near Budapest and the Stuttgart ball-bearing factory; some changes were made in the secondary targets by placing Turin at the head of the list and readjusting some of the low-ranking objectives. The destruction of Messerschmitt production still remained a prime duty of the Fifteenth; on 12 April, missions were scheduled against important centers still presumed to be in production. The important Fischamend Markt factory was attacked by 172 B-17s dropping 423 tons of GP bombs and 42.4 tons of incendiaries. In spite of intense flak, direct hits were made on three component shops, and other installations suffered damage. One bomber was shot down by antiaircraft; unfortunately, a certain percentage of the bombs fell in the residential area of Vienna.

Another task force of 134 B-24's was sent to Wiener Neustadt where a scattered but heavy concentration was achieved over about half the target area. There were direct hits on machine and locomotive shops as well as on some of the workshops. Between forty and fifty enemy planes made attacks from all angles on this task force.

The Bad Voslau aircraft assembly plant was the target for 140 bombers of the 304th Wing. A very heavy concentration inflicted severe damage on hangars and barracks near the landing field. The field itself was well covered; of the large number of planes present when the attack occurred, it was estimated in later evaluations that twenty-four were destroyed, seven probably destroyed, and five damaged. Six bombers were lost at this target. The final phase of the operation occurred when 107 Liberators dispatched without escort bombed the Zagreb airdrome and marshalling yards. The bombing was good with only one bomber lost.

   The following day, April 13, 1944, was a big one in the history of the
Fifteenth's operations. Attacks were planned against a series of important
POINTBLANK targets. High on the priority list was the aircraft production complex at Gyor, Hungary. This plant was engaged in producing the
Me-109; it was believed that no less than 40 per month were coming from
the assembly factory located at the Gyor airfield. The destruction of this
plant would reduce to seventy-five the entire monthly production of single-
engine fighters being produced within the range of the Fifteenth Air Force.
In addition to this important target, there were others that needed attention. Previous attacks at seriously damaged the Dana Components plant,
but it was believed that further demolition was necessary. Another objective
was the Budapest/Tokol airfield, which was thought to be assembling the
components from the Dana plant. At the Budapest/Vecses, Hungary, airfield extensive modification and repair facilities were available to the GAF.
In the opinion of the Fifteenth's bombing exports, "the destruction of the
Dana complex and the Vecses depot should reduce by two-thirds the total
current production of Me-210's and Me-410's of the enemy."

   To destroy these important sources of GAF production and repair, the
Fifteenth mounted one its largest missions of heavy bombers to date. On 13
April some 814 fighters and bombers were airborne in a three-phase operation. \ The Gyor factory and airfield were attacked by 103 flying Fortresses
that dropped 385.74 tons with excellent results. Practically all installations
were hit, and the landing field was well post-holed; additionally, nine enemy
aircraft were claimed as destroyed on the ground. The Gyor task force was
aggressively attacked by 20 to 30 German fighters that approached the rear
formations firing rockets up to within 160 yards as they came. They then
broke below the bombers and reformed to attack the second wave. The
Budapest/Vecses airdrome was bombed by 121 B-24's that wrought considerable damage to installations and played havoc with the large number of
aircraft parked on the landing ground. The main buildings were hit by 100
lb. bombs, which formed a heavy concentration in the southwest part of the
field; of the 130 aircraft present, 69 were believed damaged or destroyed.
The Budapest/Tokol airdrome was similarly bombed with light explosives
and fragmentation bombs by 124 aircraft. Installations were well covered,
with about forty-four planes on the field believed destroyed. The Dana

Repulogepyar aircraft factory near Budapest was bombed by 107 Liberators; the photos showed a good distribution of bombs over the factory area and direct hits on four assembly buildings.

The German fighters put up a good defense of these important targets. The Luftwaffe called in all types of attack planes, and Me-109's, -210's, -110's, FW-190's, and Ju-38's were sighted. All the formations ran into opposition, but the last unit over the Budapest area, the 304th Wing, had the most trouble. Twin-engine planes stayed out of range of the bombers' guns and fired rockets into the formations, while single-engine fighters concentrated on stragglers, cripples, and separated units. Eighteen bombers and three fighters were lost in the different phases of the operation. The destruction among enemy planes was heavy. Conservatively, it was estimated that at least 70 planes had been destroyed on the ground; fighter and bomber air claims were 43-13-15.

For the next few days the Fifteenth continued its attacks on airdromes and similar installations. On the 16th, medium-sized forces struck the airdromes at Turnu-Severin and Belgrade, inflicting some damage but leaving the fields still usable. On the same day, a larger force of 103 Fortresses attacked the Belgrade/Rogozarski fighter aircraft factory as a secondary target when the primary was found covered by cloud. The main concentration did not fall on the target but landed on the neighboring Zemun airfield, Yugoslavia; there was one direct hit on the southeast part of the factory.

The same Belgrade targets were hit again on the 17th. The Rogozarski factory was hit by a small force with some success. Weather almost prevented the attack on the Zemun airdrome, but 34 bombers managed to get through, dropping 7,925 fragmentation bombs that destroyed 4 airplanes and set fire to some hangars. A raid on the Ikarus aircraft factory showed no hits in the target area; unfortunately, the bombs fell in the residential part of Belgrade. This phase of counter-air operations ended on the following day when fighter sweeps were scheduled for the aerodromes in the Udine area. Bad weather held some of the units back, but 20 P-38's managed to strafe as planned.

The Eighth had been held up by both a poor flying weather and also a CROSSBOW mission (attacks against rocket launching sites, also called NOBALL), but on 18 April, the Bomber Command scheduled an operation against targets in the Berlin area. No enemy opposition occurred during the penetration or withdrawal, but a short sharp fight occurred at the target area. Choosing the time and place with rare discrimination, the enemy suddenly hurled 100 single-engine fighters at a formation whose units had been separated by weather conditions and were too split up to receive adequate fighter protection. In the words of an official report, "This was the advantage for which the enemy had been waiting. He saw and exploited it with split-second timing to the tune of at least 10 B-17's. Our fighters did not even see it happen."

The Arado aircraft plant at Rathenow was bombed with very good results by 121 B-24's.; equally satisfactory were the results at the Luneburg airdrome. Two heavy patterns fell across the target area with numerous hits on hangars, refueling points, a compass-swinging base, and a machine-gun range. The main concentration at Oranienburg/Annahof airdrome in Germany fell west of the field; some hits were scored on the Heinkel assembly plant, and 8 Me-177's were believed destroyed or damaged. At the Oranienburg/Germendorf airfield, 148 B-17's dropped 101 tons of GP bombs and 173 tons of incendiaries; however, no large fires were started and the main installations were not seriously damaged. The Arado plant at Brandenburg was raided by a small force with undisclosed results, and thirteen Forts dropped bombs on the Perleberg airdrome, scoring hits on three medium-sized hangars. The forces involved in the 18 April missions totaled 501 B-17's, and 275 B-24's. Bomber losses came to 19 planes and claims were low, being only 16-6-7.

Airfields and FW-190 plants were the main targets for the next day's operations (19 April). A large force, 759 airborne, was sent against the targets, which the enemy well defended. The Kassel/Bettenhausen FW-190 components factory was successfully bombed by 52 B-17's, and large fires were seen as the bombers retired from the target. At Kassel/Waldau, plant one of the FW-190 assembly plant was severely damaged.   Eleven important installations received hits, and one assembly building was set on fire.

Liberators were dispatched against the airdromes at Eschwege, Lippstadt, Werl, Paderborn, and Gutersloh; good results were obtained due to the medium altitude at which the bombing took place. However, the raids on Gutersloh were less satisfactory. Only five bombers were lost during the missions of the day.

While the Eighth was thus concentrating on the factories and airfields, certain important changes in the Fifteenth's priorities took place. The fighter assembly plant at the Turin, which had been suspended from the priority list, was reinstated in a lower position so that it could be attacked should there be large numbers of aircraft at the factory field. It was decided airfields with concentrations of operational aircraft should be given high priority, although the choice was to be left to the commands. High priority was given fields and factories making the new of jet-propelled aircraft.

Several former high-priority targets were suspended: these were the factories at Augsburg, Oberpfaffenhofen, and Aschersleben. The fighter aircraft assembly at Gotha was reinstated due to the presence of a large number of Me-110's on its field.

The new target priorities sent out two days later were as follows:

1. Wiener Neustadt
2. Bad Voslau
3. Brasov
4. Schwechat
5. Belgrade/Ikarus
6. Turin
7. Varese

Fischamend, Gyor, and Rogozarski at Belgrade were removed from the first priority because of the severe damage inflicted on them. The secondary priority included the following:

1. Klagenfurt
2. Steyr-Daimler-Puch (Steyr)
3. Gyor assembly plant
4. Budapest/ Tokol airfields

Fillers for when weather prevented action against the first and second priorities were two minor branches of the Wiener Neustadt complex and other identified components factories and repair works. A special point was made of the importance of airfields, especially when connected with repair and related functions. In view of the declining state of the Luftwaffe such installations were far more important as targets than before.

#

To translate the new instructions into action, the XV Bomber Command planned a large operation against the airfields and aircraft factories at Bad Voslau, Schwechat, and Werner Neustadt on 23 April; an attack on the Wiener Neustadt Nord airfield was also scheduled. These objectives were some of the most important within the range of the Fifteenth Air Force - Schwechat was especially vital. As has been pointed out, it was the center of important jet developments; since a plan for bombing the Me-217 plant in Poland had fallen through, Schwechat was now the sole producer of this twin-engine fighter-bomber. Both Bad Voslau and the Wiener Neustadt Word airfield housed large numbers of newly assembled Me-109 planes and offered an excellent target for fragmentation bombs.

The attack was mounted approximately as planned. A total of 956 aircraft were airborne and dropped 1,292.5 tons of bombs. In the aerial battle, 175 to 200 enemy planes engaged the bombers. Three fighters and thirteen bombers were lost, and claims of 51-16-32 were made by the American forces. The Wiener Neustadt factory was to have been attacked by 222 B-17's, but some aborted—only 171 reached the target. The bombing was very successful. Severe damage was inflicted on a large machine shop, and the main shop showed fresh roof damage. The east extension of the factory received two direct hits in the center and probably received considerable blast damage. The assembly shop was probably struck directly, for the roof contained large holes.

At Schwechat, 140 bombers scored direct hits on the two assembly shop, a workshop, two flight hangars and some barracks. Bad Voslau received a heavy load of 261.75 tons of 500-lb. bombs and 12,550 x 20-lb. fragmentation bombs. Later photos show the airdrome and all principal installations heavily hit, and General Twining characterized the results as "superb." The most badly damaged buildings included eight hangars, some office buildings, barracks, the boiler house, and maintenance bays. Some 21 aircraft were damaged on the field, and the northwest half of the airdrome was completely covered by 500-lb. and fragmentation bombs.

The Nord airdrome at Wiener Neustadt was bombed by a small force of Liberators dropping 3,642 x 20-lb. fragmentation bombs from 23,500 feet. A total of 67 planes were widely dispersed on the field, with only 10 Me-109's considered destroyed. No fresh damage to the installations was visible. The next day the Ikarus aircraft factory at Belgrade was hit by 56.5 tons of high explosive. Only partial coverage of the target was secured, but some bombs fell on the Zemun station and marshalling yards.

As April drew to a close, the tempo of POINTBLANK operations was stepped up, and missions against the GAF took place almost daily. On 23 April, the VIII Fighter Command carried out a big fighter sweep and fighter-bomber operations against German-held airdromes in northern France, Belgium, and Germany. Nine groups of P-38's, P-47's, and P-51's were involved in the raids, and two other groups acted as escorts. There was no enemy opposition in the air, but seven fighters were lost to flak. The pilots claimed eleven enemy planes destroyed and twenty-four damaged as a result of the ground strafing.

The VIII Bomber Command took over the attack on the following day when 754 bombers and 892 fighters were airborne in a mission against several GAF targets. Of the three divisions involved, the only real opposition of the day developed against the 1st, which who attacked by more than 100 single-engine fighters in the Landsburg-Oberpfaffenhofen area. At this point the 1st Division's bombers were considerably spread out, and the two groups of escorting Mustangs had their hands full. In spite of all their efforts, 20 B-17's were lost to enemy aircraft in this phase of the action.

Several targets in the vicinity of Friedrichshafen were attacked by 211 B-17's. The largest gear-cutting factory in Germany, the Friedrichshafen Zahnredfabrik, was severely damaged, and the home airfield of the Dornier aircraft company complex received an excellent bomb pattern which inflicted damage on important buildings. The largest task force of the operation (120 Liberators) hit the repair and equipment depot at Gablingen with 222 tons. The bombing was carried out from the relatively medium altitude of 16,700 to 19,000 feet. The incendiaries started large fires and there were explosions; three of six large hangars received direct hits, two hangars were gutted by fire. The three-wave attack on Oberpfaffenhofen was quite successful, although the bombs of the second wave fell outside the target area. Nevertheless, a photo reconnaissance mission showed that every major building was now damaged to some degree. At least twelve aircraft parked on the field were destroyed or damaged. At Erding, a good pattern fell on the airfield where fourteen planes were damaged, but the bombs missed the equipment depot which was one of the objectives. A total of 40 bombers were lost in the different phases of this operation, but to compensate for this, the very high claims of 103-26-43 were filed by bomber and fighter crews.

On the 25th, both the Eighth and Fifteenth were active. The Fifteenth sent 114 B-24's to attack the Turin factory with fair success, while the Eighth scheduled a series of medium-sized missions against French airfields. The largest operation was directed against the Dijon/Longvic airfield where 298 tons of BP and 40.1 tons of incendiary bombs were dropped with good results; only two hangars were left undamaged. Other fields attacked were at Metz/Frescati and Haney/Essey. The increasing emphasis on airfields in the operations of both strategic air forces was due to a suspected change in German production methods. It was now clear the enemy was dispersing his planes to fields where repair facilities were known to exist. However, it was suspected that at some of these fields, particularly those near already destroyed assembly centers, a small amount of assembly work might be taking place. As a result, airfields were now being watched even more carefully for new activities than were the big production complexes.

A significant mission took place on the 26th when 10 combat wings of the VIII Bomber Command were dispatched to attack aircraft plants and airfields in Germany. A low cloud cover prevented visual bombing of the primaries, but five B-17 wings attacked the secondary target of Brunswick using radar. The noteworthy aspects of the operation were the facts that it was completely unopposed; for the first time, there were no bomber losses. Although the weather was poor for bombing, it was not so bad as to preclude flying; therefore, it does not explain the failure of the GAF to rise to the defense of important German targets.

The next two days were devoted to attacking NOBALL targets and airfields. On the 27th, two B-17 combat wings found their assigned airfields cloud-covered; consequently, Le Culot and the Ostend/Middelkerke airfields in Belgium were bombed with fair results. Approximately 300 tons of fragmentation, high-explosive, and incendiary bombs were dropped. Another task force of three B-17 combat wings successfully hit the fields at Nancy/Essey and Toul/Croix de Metz with 446 tons. The only opposition in these operations came from flak. The following day, along with missions against installations in the Pas de Calais, a fore of 118 Fortresses went out against the airfields, dropping a total of 310.7 tons from medium altitude with very good results. The destruction of hangars was especially effective, and fourteen barracks received direct hits.

Any belief that the extremely light enemy opposition of the last few days was symptomatic of the early death of the Luftwaffe ended abruptly during the heavy attack on Berlin of 29 April. Although not a POINTBLANK mission, it is worth describing in detail because it affords an excellent illustration of GAF tactics in defense of a vital target. The American bomber forces, some 679 planes strong with 838 protecting fighters, approached the target along a Zuider Zee-Hanover line in three massive formations led by the 3d Division with the 1st following, and the 2d in the unpopular position of "tail-end Charlie."

As the 3d Division led the bombers across Holland, one combat wing left the formation and continued eastward on a route of its own, which took it well outside the fighter escort (the reports of the mission do not explain the reason for the strange behavior of this combat wing). The enemy fighter controller immediately took note of this error, and when this wing reached the area around Magdeburg, Germany where the first fighter Staffeln were assembling, it was pounced upon by seventy-five enemy planes attacking in waves of fifteen to twenty aircraft. In its undefended condition, the wing was at a great disadvantage and quickly lost fifteen bombers.

Meanwhile, the bombers were streaming across the Hanover area while the German fighter controller held back his fighters waiting for the proper moment to strike. The 3rd and 1st Divisions were well escorted and allowed to pass unchallenged. But the 2d Division, which was following in the rear position, was escorted only by one group of P-47s and one group of P-38s. When the division reached Celle, the P-47 group had to turn back, thus leaving 233 bombers supported by 37 Mustangs. Here was the moment. As the Thunderbolts retired, three Staffeln drew off the remaining Mustangs and sixty to seventy fighters attacked steadily until the bombers reached Berlin.

Once over Berlin the battle swung our way. Originally, about 150 enemy fighters had concentrated in this area, but when the combat wing of the 3rd Division became separated, about half the GAF fighters left the Berlin sector to engage them. Consequently, when our formations reached the city, now strengthened by additional fighter escorts which had joined them at Celle, the odds were too unequal and the GAF refused to join battle. Instead, the fighter controller decided to concentrate his strength for a final blow at the already harassed 2d Division as it withdrew.

At this time the 2nd was about 30 minutes behind schedule, and when its attendant P-47's had to leave because of fuel shortages, it had already missed its rendezvous with the P-38's, which were to escort it home. Consequently, when the 2d Division passed over the Hanover area and was on its way home, it was again attacked by about 100 fighters, most of which had been withheld from combat at the target area. As a result of these careful calculations by the German fighter controller, the 2d Division alone lost 25 bombers, and the total cost of the day's operations was 63 bombers and 13 fighters. Eighth Air Force claims were 87-28-45.

The final operations of the month for the Eighth Air Force consisted of airdrome missions. The Lyon/Bron field was attacked very successfully by 114 B-17's and 110 Struck at the Clermont-Ferrand/Aulnat base with equally good results. Fighter sweeps were carried out across the Tours and Orleans/Bricy fields, and a few planes were destroyed on the ground.

April was an important month in POINTBLANK operations. With improving weather, both the Eighth and the Fifteenth were able to apply an almost continuous pressure on the GAF. For both forces, airdromes were increasingly important; at the same time, a heavy toll was taken of the Luftwaffe in the air. The Eighth Air Force claimed a total of 764 enemy planes in the air and on the ground. Similar figures for the Fifteenth amounted to 653.

The Eighth turned its attention again to FW-190 and twin-engine fighter production, while the Fifteenth was believed to seriously upset the balance of the Messerschmitt production. Together the Eighth and the Fifteenth made it clear that there was no place in the Reich safe from these two strategic air forces.

To judge by the defense the enemy was capable of getting up at certain times and places, there was little outward indication that the Luftwaffe was nearing collapse. However, these shows of strength may have been more apparent than real. Missions over northwestern France, Belgium, and Holland were apt to see little air opposition; attacks occasionally failed to produce any Luftwaffe reaction. By April, it was the opinion of the Combined Operational Planning Committee that the Germans had ceased to defend certain areas or even certain targets as such. Rather, they were attempting to exploit weakness in the bomber escort that might develop. In addition to the heavy flax concentrations in the Ruhr, along the routes north to the Hanover-Berlin line and east to the Frankfort-Regensburg line, increasingly larger formations were entering the Reich along these lines causing concentrations of enemy fighters to appear on the forward or rear of the formations.

Opposition to the Fifteenth Air Force was probably a little lighter than to the Eighth. The XV Bomber Command was likely to be intercepted by fighters based in northern Italy around the head of the Adriatic or located in the Klagenfurt-Graz area in Austria. However, continued and effective bombing of those fields probably considerably reduced their effectiveness. During April, the Fifteenth lost 194 bombers, or 2.2 percent of the effective sorties.

Just at the end of April and the beginning of May, a thorough reshuffling of targets and priorities occurred for both strategic air forces. Many of the objectives, which had long been familiar to the pilots and bombardiers of the XV Bomber Command, were suspended. In south Germany, the factories and airfields at Augsburg, Lechfeld, Regensburg, Landsburg and others were removed from the priority list. Still active targets were base facilities at Munich and the supply (Me-410) and component (Do-217) center at Neuaubing. In the Steyr-Vienna area, the following targets, long famous in the annuls of the XV Bomber Command, were taken from the active list: Fischamend, Schwechat, Bad Voslau, and the Steyr Walzalagerwerke. The Werke I and II at Wiener Neustadt, and numerous airdromes, were still open for attack. Also kept on the list were Steyr-Daimler-Puch, the Me-109 component plant at Klagenfurt, and the Graz airdrome.

In northern Italy, the suspended targets were the Reggio Emilia aircraft factory and the ball-bearing plants at Turin and Villar Perosa. The Macchi factory at Varese, the airdrome at Milan, and the Turin factory could still be attached.

In the Balkan area, the suspensions were fewer as they were confined to the Rogozarski plant at Zemun (Yugoslavia) and the Hungarian wagon works at Gyor. All the other Balkan POINTBLANK targets were to be attacked. For the Eighth Air Force, important targets still remaining were at Sorau, Tutow, Bernburg, Cottbus, and Kreising.

Basic priorities for both air forces were readjusted on 6 May. It will be recalled that late in March, some questions had been raised concerning the bombing of targets in southeastern Europe and their relation to the POINTBLANK program. With the invasion of Europe nearing, it was now definitely stated that POINTBLANK had priority over these targets, except when weather prevented attacks on POINTBLANK objectives. For the Fifteenth, the objectives were: (1) to support the land battle in Italy; (2) POINTBLANK; (3) rail communications in southern France; and (4) targets in the Balkans. It was further stated that in southeastern Europe, communications were the priority objectives; however, when tactical considerations were paramount, the Fifteenth was authorized to combine attacks on oil refineries with communications.

The Eighth was still authorized to consider POINTBLANK as the number one priority, but second place went to railway centers in occupied countries, and third was assigned to airdromes in German-held territory. (The exact definition of POINTBLANK was never clearly established in current usage. Sometimes airdromes were considered a part of it, and sometimes they were placed in a separate category. Obviously, attacks on them were a part of the war against the Luftwaffe; nonetheless, this was the start of a new and intense offensive against airfields so that the GAF will not have time to recover them before D-Day.)

Bad weather hampered operations in northwest Europe during the first week in May. The Eighth sent a small force against airfields at Bois de l'Enfer, Paix, Montdidier, and Roye/Amy. on 1 May but little was accomplished. A big mission was scheduled for the 4th and was actually airborne, but heavy clouds caused a recall of the bombers. Since some of the leading formations had already reached the Dutch coast, 43 B-17's dropped their bombs on the Bergen/Alkmaar airfield in Holland. The results were probably good, as heavy black smoke arose from this target. There were no bomber claims or losses.

The Fifteenth went into operations against airdromes on the 6th. A large force was sent against Rumanian targets and 161 Fortresses of the 5th Wing were detailed to bomb the Brasov aircraft factory and airdrome. Some 235 tons of 500-lb. GP bombs were dropped along with 84.55 tons of fragmentation bombs with good results . The frags covered the airdrome and landing area, and the high explosives landed on four hangars, two workshops and the main administration buildings. Six aircraft on the field were destroyed and four were damaged.

After several missions against NOBALL rocket targets, Berlin and other cities, and communication centers, the Eighth returned to counter-air targets on the 9th. A large armada of 727 bombers was dispatched to strike at three marshalling yards and eight airfields in France and Belgium. There was very little enemy opposition, for it appeared that the Germans anticipated a deep penetration from so formidable an array and were concentrating farther inland. Only one formation of bombers operating in the vicinity of Antwerp encountered active opposition; the remainder were practically unchallenged. The airdromes bombed away, and the number of planes attacking were as follows: Saint Dizier (74) Robinson, Thionville (54), Juvincourt-et-Damary (72), Saint-Trond (110), Florennes (106), Laon/Athies (127), Laon/Couvron (124), and Lille/Vendeville (19 as a secondary). Bombing results were considered uniformly good.

On the 13th, the Eighth planned a large mission against German aircraft production at the extreme limits of the bombers' radius of operation. Attacks were scheduled against the Focke-Wulf plants at Kreising and

Posen in Poland, and against the airfield and airpark at Tutow. Unfortunately, weather seriously interfered with the bombing. The overcast at Kreising and Posen prevented bombing, and the bombers assigned to these objectives attacked targets of opportunity. Only at Tutow was the bombing carried out as planned; here, 226 B-24's reached the area and bombed with fairly good success on the eastern part of the field. Only 12 bombers were lost in those deep penetrations and total claims were 62-5-16.

Airfields were still high on the priorities of the Fifteenth. Piacenza and Reggio Emelia airdromes were attacked on 14 May by 141 and 75 heavy bombers, respectively, while P-38's strafed the air bases at Aviano, Villaorba and Rivolta. The bombing was satisfactory and the fighters claimed nineteen enemy aircraft were destroyed on the ground. On the same day, other fighters of the Fifteenth strafed airfields at Villa Franca, Forli, Reggio Emilia, and Modena. At Forli, several hangars were set on fire.

Meanwhile a new list of priorities was being worked out and on 15 May, General Eaker sent it to General Twining. As first priority, the following targets were listed:

1. Wollersdorf airdrome and airpark, Wiener Neustadt
2. Components factory at Atzgersdorf, Austria
3. Dornier factory at Oberpfaffenhofen
4. Munich/Neubiberg airpark
5. Vecses airdrome
6. Zwolfaxing airdrome, Austria
7. Munich/Weis airpark
8. Dornier factory at Neuaubing
9. Graz/Thalerhof airdrome

The secondary priority contained the following objectives:

1. Erding airdrome and park, Germany
2. Budaors airdrome in Hungry
3. Muller ball-bearing factory at Nuremberg
4. Extension of the Wiener Neustadt complex at Klagenfurt

5. Steyr-Daimler-Puch plant at Steyr
6. Wiener Neustadt extension at Neunkirchen, Germany
7. Wiener Neustadt extension at Pottendorf, Austria
8. Wiener Neustadt extension at Ebreichsdorf, Austria
9. Wiener Neustadt extension at Voslau
10. Steyr-Daimler-Puch plant at Graz/Neudorf, Austria

The third priority dealt with fourteen airdromes

\#

The final ten days in May was a transition period where POINTBLANK was giving way to OVERLORD. As the time for invasion drew near, every effort was made to increase the pressure on the Luftwaffe. Both the Eighth and Fifteenth were extremely active against airdromes, especially the Eighth since it was under the imperative necessarily of reaching and destroying the fields from which the GAF might launch counterattacks on the Anglo-American landing forces.

On 20 May, the Eighth led off with attacks on two French airfields and one aircraft repair center. Reims/Champagne was attacked by sixty-six Liberators with very good results. Several direct hits were scored on hangars and the west side of the landing area. The Paris, France Orly airfield received 249 tons from 90 B-17's, and a good coverage of the target resulted. Four aiming points were assigned at the Villacoublay aircraft facilities and all were hit. Bursts blanketed the Morane-Saulnier aircraft assembly works in France, and there were hits on ten factory buildings. Some seventy bursts fell in the hangar and barracks area at the west corner of the plant. Another large group of bombs fell on the Nord aircraft works causing considerable damage.

On the 23rd, a very large force of 1,045 heavy bombers escorted by 1,185 fighters were dispatched to attack marshalling yards and airdromes in France. Enemy air opposition was practically nil, but the weather made up for the lack of German activity. Only 815 bombers were able to attack, and ground haze rendered target identification uncertain. As a result, the bombing varied from poor to good. The airfields attacked were at Saarbrucken, Metz, Epinal, Bayon, Chaumont, Etampes, Chateaudun, Caen/ Carpiquet, Bourges, and Orleans/Bricy.

Probably the most successful attack was against the Orleans/Bricy field; here, 391 tons of GP and 70.6 tons of incendiary bombs were dropped from relatively medium altitudes. Ammunition dumps, fueling pits, dispersal areas, and hangars were all hit.

The next day a large force of 447 bombers was dispatched to Berlin, having been preceded by attacks on Orly, Melun, Creil, and Poixby by 440 bombers. Opposition was fierce and thirty-three bombers are lost.

While the Eighth was paving the way for the imminent invasion of the Continent, the Fifteenth was beginning its own last-phase attack on airfields and factories. Six hundred and twenty-plus B-17's and B-24's attacked the Atzgersdorf aircraft components factory, while 135 attacked the airfields at Neunkirchen, Munchendorf, Graz, Wollersdorf, Bad Voslau and Zagreb. Only ninety-three hit the air bases and with poor results; two bombed the Graz with undisclosed results. Enemy fighter opposition was especially heavy against the Bad Voslau force, downing six bombers for the day.

On the 27th of May, almost 700 B-17's and B-24's, with P-38 and P-51 escorts, bombed the marshalling yards at Avignon, Montpellier-Frejorgues, Nimes, Marseilles-Blancarde, and Marseille-Saint Charles, all of which were in France, the airfield at Salon-de-Provence, France, and port of Razanac, Yugoslavia.

Two hundred and sixty-five heavy bombers were sent out against two French airdromes. Montpellier-Frejorgues was hit by 262 tons with very good results. The main installations such as hangars, personnel quarters, administration buildings, and transport facilities were all hit, and the north-east landing ground and runway were well cratered. The Salon de Provence air base, which had been bombed during the critical days of the Anzio beachhead, was also attacked during the raid on Montpellier. Strike photos revealed direct hits on various hangars, 2 hits on the repair shops, 5 hits and 4 near misses on the administration building, and some 130 craters on the northwest landing area. One B-24 failed to return from this mission.

The Eighth Air Force concluded the month's operations by running five tremendous missions (27-31 May) against German aircraft, oil and trans-portation targets. Over 900 bombers were airborne in each operation. On

27 May, forces totaling 991 bombers were dispatched to northwest France to bomb certain targets largely connected with rail communications; however, two small task forces attacked aero-engine plants. The Junkers aero-engine plant at Strasbourg was hit by fifty-three Fortresses with good results, and an engine factory near Metz was bombed by sixty-nine Liberators with results estimated at fair to good. There was only moderate GAF opposition. Nineteen heavy bombers were shot down and seven fighters were lost. Claims against the enemy testified to the laxness of the defense, being only 36-4-13.

The next day, the pressure on the Reich was increased when 1,027 heavy bombers went out against all refineries, aircraft works, and a military depot in central Germany. The attack was make by two task forces: one, which opened the battle, made a diversionary raid southeast, then turned north to bomb Cologne and withdrew. The enemy was not deceived by this thrust, proceeding to concentrate 350 single-engine and 50 twin-engine fighters in the Magdeburg area to oppose the huge main force, which was rapidly approaching from the Guider Zee in the direction of Wittingen, Germany. Upon reaching this point, the formations separated to bomb their various targets; at this moment, the German fighter controller threw his heavy concentration at the tail of the 1st Division and the leading formations of the 3d. By concentrating his forces, the enemy was able to achieve a temporary superiority which saturated the fighter defense and brought down eighteen bombers. The rest of the formation was practically unopposed from the air.

Most of the bombing effort was not directed against the German aircraft industry; small forces raided a Junkers aircraft assembly and engine works at Dessau and airfields at Brandis and Wustensachsen, Germany. Owing to the interference of haze, smoke, and cloud, the results were generally poor. Losses in the whole operation mounted to thiryt-two bombers and fourteen fighters. Although the Luftwaffe offered severe opposition in only one phase of the engagement, the battle was fierce with many German planes shot down. Total claims against the enemy came to 69-31-36.

The Eighth did better against the German aircraft industry on the 29th. Two hundred and fifty-one Fortresses were dispatched against the Me-109 plants of the Erla complex in the Leipzig area, and the Ju-88 assembly plant. The bombing here was rated fair to good. Another force of 299 B-17's attacked Focke-Wulf facilities, including the components plant at Posen and the assembly factories at Cottbus and Krzesiny, Poland, and Sorau. The results at Krzesiny and Sorau were good, but the bombing at Cottbus and Posen was less accurate. The opposition appeared to be confused by a double-thrust approach with one formation coming up over the North Sea and another apparently headed straight for Berlin. Consequently, the Luftwaffe was scattered and its defense was effective at only one point. Total bomber losses nonetheless came to 34 planes, with claims against the GAF at 79-14-21.

The next day another massive formation was dispatched against airfields and factories, marshalling yards, and NOBALL installations along the French coast. All the bombers followed approximately the same route until they reached the Dutch-German border. The 1st Division continued deep into the Reich to attack certain aircraft factories, while the other formations fanned out to bomb "shallow" targets. The Junkers parent plant at Dessau, Germany, was bombed by 79 B-17's, causing extensive damage. A machine shop, a workshop, and seven engine-testing beds, as well as offices and storehouses, were completely destroyed. The FW-190 plant at Oschersleben, which had been often attacked and promptly repaired, received the attention of 51 B-17's that inflicted extensive injury. At least ten direct hits were scored on a large machine shop, and other installations were damaged. The Halberstadt Junkers plant lost its boiler house, several office buildings, and a large workshop. The recreation center, storehouse, motor transport yard, canteen, fire station, and an office building were partially destroyed. The local airfield was attacked by forty-eight bombers able to cover the southern half of the landing area with bursts.

One of the largest task forces of the 30 May mission was sent to bomb the airfield at Rotenburg, Germany. Six heavy concentrations of high explosives and incendiaries were dropped by 147 B-24's in the target area, and the objective was blanketed by bursts. At the airfield and seaplane station at Zwischenahn, Germany a good concentration was secured on the southern part of the field, and similar results were achieved at Oldenburg. The GAF stations at Diepholz and Handorf were bombed by small forces with satisfactory results. Only the 1st Division ran into any opposition, and this was doubtless due to its deep penetration since the Luftwaffe now seldom concerned itself with operations over Belgium, Holland, and northwest France. Owing to the fact that a part of the division got six minutes ahead of schedule and lost some of its escort, the GAF was able to attack with some success. Twelve bombers were lost during the day, but at considerable cost to the enemy. American bomber and fighter claims were 60-7-9.

The final mission of the month was largely devoted to marshalling yards and bridges; however, small units struck the airfields at Luxeuil-les-Bains, France and Gilze-Rijen in Holland. A raid on an aero-engine factory at had to be canceled because of weather. There were no claims or losses.

While the Eighth was thus making history over the roofless Festung Europa, the Fifteenth was finishing up its attack on German fighter production in southern Germany. Unlike the Eighth, tactical considerations did not force the Fifteenth to concentrate on fighter airdromes. The early attacks on airfields had apparently been effective, for a comparison of the photo reconnaissance of 13 April with one of 29 May showed a great decline in aircraft on fields within the Budapest area. On the former date, there were 123 single-engine fighters, 26 Me-110's, and 101 Me-410's at Budaors, Vecses, and Tokol. On 29 May there were present at these same fields (plus two others) 12 single-engine fighters and 29 Me-110's and -410's. Of special importance was the fact that the 29 May reconnaissance showed no activity of any kind at the Tokol airfield and factory.

On 29 May, the Fifteenth carried out a big operation, which virtually gave the Coup de Grace to the Wiener Neustadt Werk I. This target was attacked by 104 Liberators dropping 219.75 tons with devastating effect. The photographs showed the hangar and factory area were completely saturated with bursts. Many aircraft were destroyed or damaged on the ground and there was considerable blast damage; at least ten direct hits were seen on the hangars. Another task force of 126 Liberators bombed the Atzgersdorf aircraft factory. Smoke made the assessment of damage difficult, but three direct hits were located on the main factory buildings and the area between the main building and the factory road was blanketed with bursts. A third task force of 304 planes was dispatched to the Wollersdorf, Austria, airdrome. This target was smothered by 740.35 tons of different types of explosives. Direct hits occurred on five hangars on the north side and six hangars on the south perimeter. Workshops, storage buildings, administration offices, and barracks were all covered with bursts; oil fires and explosions were evident in several places. That this was a vital target was evident from the GAF reaction. Some 150 fighters attempted to intercept the bombers, and, failing this, concentrated on stragglers and bombers wounded by flak. Five bombers were shot down in the air battle and two more were missing; the enemy lost eighteen planes in the air and twelve on the ground, according to the claims of the bomber and fighter crews. Some 829 heavy bombers attacked targets that day. A total of eighteen bombers failed to return to their bases from all these operations.

This operation was so effective that it was believed possible to completely eliminate the remaining members of the Wiener Neustadt complex in one more operation. Four units were still suspected of performing important functions in Messerschmitt production: the Wels airfield and aircraft factory, the Neudorf factory, the spinning mill, and the carpet factory. The Wels plant was formerly engaged in the repair of bombers, but it was believed that this had been suspended for some time; a reconnaissance mission earlier in May showed 110 planes present of which a large number were Me-109's and -110's. This further substantiated the belief that the plant was engaged in fighter production or repair. It was known that Neudorf was engaged in the manufacture of aircraft components; it was believed that, specifically, these were wings and fuselages for Messerschmitt planes. Less was understand about the other two facilities, although the former had certainly received some of the Wiener Neustadt dispersed production. It was now thought that these functions included some of the metal-shaping work and fuselage sub-assembling formerly done in Werk II of the Wiener Neustadt plant. The other plant had been converted into a component plant for fighter aircraft, although it was not clear which components were being produced. The plant was suitable for making small parts and carrying out the subassembly of fuselages, as it was certainly considered an important unit.

Consequently, a combined day and night operation on a very large scale was organized by the Fifteenth against the dispersed component plants of the Wiener Neustadt complex, and several other targets. The first phase began shortly after midnight on 30 May when 38 Wellingtons were dispatched to bomb the airdromes at low altitude. The bombing was well concentrated with many strings across the field accompanied by explosions and fires. A few hours after sunrise, the next phase began when 481 B-24s and 56 B-17s, accompanied by 137 P-38s and 95 P-51s, went out against the factories

With the end of May in sight, the emphasis was shifted from POINT-BLANK to other targets. Although it was felt that the destruction of the Luftwaffe had not been completely carried out, oil and transportation stations were to become the top-ranking priority targets in the months to come. Once the Normandy beachhead was established, tactical considerations further reduced POINTBLANK to a lower position on the Eighth's priorities; however, the landing on the coast of southern France would still impact the Fifteenth.

#

For the May both strategic forces established new records nevertheless, the GAF continued to absorb these undoubtedly enormous loses. It no longer controlled the air but could only raise resistance when errors in navigation or weather conditions carried the bombers out of the fighter screen, and on D-day, it was nil or completely inferior to the primary functions of a strategic air force, but in spite of all this it continued to grow. Problematically, the production of German fighter planes slowly crept up even after the devastating raids of February 1944, and the production of Me-109's and FW-190's was estimated by the Air Ministry at 925, the highest figure yet recorded for the output of these fighters. Did this mean that POINT-BLANK was a complete or even partial failure? Under the circumstances, was it possible to destroy the Luftwaffe? Perhaps these questions, fundamental though they be, cannot be answered positively at present. However, the next and concluding chapter of this study will attempt to summarize the latest information on the results of the attack on the Luftwaffe, and the reader may, if he wishes, work out his own answers to the questions.

7

CONCLUSION

Before attempting to sum of the results, the reader needs to recall certain problems connected with the writing of this study. One of the principal difficulties was not so much a lack of information as its variety and diversity. For example, statistical information on the bomb load, number of planes dispatched, number of bombings, and number of those lost on each mission can be found in the unit histories, the tactical mission reports, the bomber command operational narratives, and in the files of the Office of Statistical Control, Headquarter, AAF. Quite often, all these sources gave different sets of figures for the same operation; furthermore, there was often disagreement as to the results of a particular bombing mission. Sometimes the overcast prevented any estimate whatsoever of the damage done; sometimes the photographs were poor because smoke or clouds got in between the lens and the target. When excellent photographs were available in quantity, the interpreters disagreed among themselves as to exactly what effect on production the destruction of a certain building would have.

Even less certainty exists in the case of German planes destroyed by our formations, on the ground, or in air combat. That such claims might be made in perfectly good faith and yet be considerably exaggerated in the excitement and stress of battle was early recognized by the AAF; as a result, great pains were taken to make the official reports as accurate as possible.

Nevertheless, American commanders such as General Doolittle admitted the unreliability of such figures, and the British frequently complained that our estimates of destroyed, probably destroyed, and damaged were far too high.

Considerable variation also exists in the estimates of German plane production. Although the RAF frequently used the Air Ministry Estimates in its planning, it was believed these were apt to be too conservative. However, when one division worked out its own estimates, G-2, the intelligence division, often disagreed with them. Finally, the leaders of the German aircraft industry themselves were apparently uncertain as to the actual number of planes they produced. Although they seemed to agree on the number made during the peak month of 1944, there was little unanimity on just when was the peak month. In view of these differences of opinion and information, the following attempt to summarize some of the results of the war against the Luftwaffe should be seen in its true and tentative aspect. These conclusions are only probabilities. They seem reasonable on the basis of the information available at the end of August 1945, but better knowledge of the facts may obviate any one of them at some future time.

With this preliminary caveat disposed, it seems possible to begin, like Descartes, with one fundamental fact: the Luftwaffe was not destroyed. Apparently, in 1943, some of the leading American air authorities were still hopeful this could be done, but by the spring of 1944, a new tone was evident. As pointed out in the previous chapter, one hear less of destroying the German fighter strength and more about containing it or at least rendering it ineffective. One high-ranking officer said quite frankly it was probably impossible to destroy it.

Not only was the Luftwaffe able to survive, but, quantitatively at least, it increased. Although the attacks of 1943 did not cause the aircraft industry much damage, the raids of February 1944 apparently caused a drop in production that may have been felt for two and one-half months. Nevertheless, the enemy managed to survive this crisis by drawing heavily on reserves, stripping the training program of planes, reducing the training time to the lowest minimum of hours, and above all, by carrying out dispersal plans already under way. Terrific difficulties were encountered: "Moving the industry underground, using every available work shop, no matter how small, every garage to produce parts, replacement of workers, moving and housing the workers ... [these] were but a few of our gargantuan tasks." Despite all those difficulties, however, production began to increase and most German authorities are in agreement that at its peak it came close to 4,000 operational types (a month) in the fall of 1944.

How was this possible in view of the tremendous weight of the AAF attack on German production? As indicated above, the dispersal of factories was undoubtedly a serious factor. But there were other considerations. If one can believe the Germans, it is possible we erred in concentrating on the airframe assemblies. Goering believed that it would have been much more effective had we bombed manufacturers of individual parts instead of the assemblies, and he cited the case of the Focke-Wulf assembly at Marienburg. This plant was largely destroyed in one highly successful raid; however, production of the FW-190 was not really hindered since it could be quickly transferred elsewhere as long as nothing interfered with the supply of important parts. Dr. Carl Fryday, chief of the Airframe Division, and Dr. Kurt W. Tank, chief engineer, test pilot, and designer of the FW-190 at the Focke-Wulf company, corroborated this evidence.

Dr. Fryday maintained that the greatest result in the February 1944 attacks occurred only when machine tools were destroyed. The attack on Leipzig was much more effective than the impressive destruction at Gotha because the machine shops at the latter plant were sparred. On the other hand, one of the attacks was considered extremely destructive because fifteen percent of the facilities for producing component parts were wiped out. These conclusions were supported by Dr. Tank, who felt the aero-engines would have been a more vulnerable objective than airframe assemblies. Goering shared this belief in the importance of the aero-engine plants, but Dr. Wilhelm Amil "Willy" Messerschmitt, designer of two famous planes bearing his name, has stated it makes no difference which is attacked first. According to him, both airframe and aero-engine plants were of equal importance.

Almost all of the German air authorities interrogated by Americans during the months following the end of the European war seemed to feel that the Luftwaffe (and incidentally the entire German war machine) could have been forced out much earlier in the oil facilities had been bombed sooner. Not only could this have stalled the Luftwaffe, but according to Field Marshal Wilhelm G. Keitel, Hitler's war minister, oil was the one industry that could not disperse to escape bombing like the aircraft industry. Likewise, transportation, when it was finally attacked by heavy forces in the latter half of 1944, broke down completely; this collapse largely nullified the intensive air dispersal of aircraft production.

It was discovered that sleeve bearings could often be substituted for other types. However, the use of plastic bearings was unsuccessful, in the opinion of Dr. Tank, but increased imports of Swiss bearings helped to offset the immediate effects of the attacks on Schweinfurt and other centers.

To summarize the results of the interruptions, most of the Germans felt that the aircraft industry was a less vital target than certain others. According to Goering, the priorities should have been as follows:

1. Synthetic oil production
2. Communications
3. Aero-engines
4. Airframe factories
5. Ball-bearing plants
6. Airfields

When Dr. Fryday was asked his opinion, he replied:

```
"After the war is done, everyone is clever. If I had to do it again,
first would be chemicals, then oil, railways and waterways. If only on
the aircraft industry, hit not assembly shops, but detail shops because
they are the most difficult to replace. They are also difficult to hit.
The second is hulls and then wings. But first of all engines, lathes,
milling machines, grinding machines."
```

Field Marshal Keitel believed the transportation network was the most decisive target in the collapse of Germany. Next to this is placed demoralization of the entire Reich and of the nation. "In this connection," he stated, "I would like to stress that the tremendous damage that was inflicted throughout Germany as a result of your air attacks was out of all proportion to the damage inflicted on armament production. There was always the possibility to disperse the production. Only the oil industry was beyond repair."

If these comments by high-ranking military and civilian authorities in the Reich suggest that the Luftwaffe might have been eliminated more quickly and more thoroughly as a factor in the war, it would be well to remember that, as Dr. Fryday said, "After the war is done, everyone is clever." The proper selection of targets for strategic bombing was a matter that received the most intensive study by both British and American authorities; doubtless the objectives attacked were chosen on the basis of the best information then available. Nor should it be assumed that the Anglo-American air offensive against the German Air Force was taken lightly in Berlin. As a matter of fact, it caused the most serious concern. In the words of an operations officer on the GAF general staff in Italy, "Had it not been that we were fighting a desperate, fanatically defensive war, our aircraft industry could have never overcome your bombings." Without the fierce air attacks by the Luftwaffe, the bombings American would have overwhelmed the industry.

When the allowance is made for the fact that production of German aircraft increased during the middle of 1944, it must also be remembered that these figures were considerably less than the goals the Germans had set for themselves. According to Dr. Tank, FW-190 production was set at 3,000 for August 1944; by September (which many Germans considered the peak month), output had only reached 2,000 per month, and it may in fact have been considerably less. (According to Dr. Hether of the Focke-Wulf company, the average monthly production of the FW-190 during 1944 was 1,000. During June, the maximum of 2,000 was achieved, but by September this had dropped back to 1,000.) Thus, there is little doubt that the POINT-BLANK offensive held down the expansion of the aircraft production to a minimum.

Another effect of the counter-air offensive was to create a serious pilot shortage in the Luftwaffe, which may explain why so few of the aircraft produced in 1944 became actually operational. Naturally, the training program was at once affected. Training of pilots, once a four year affair, was reduced to 44 air hours by 1944. (It is only fair to state that Dr. Tank believed the oil shortage played an important part in reducing the number of air hours required in training.) The growing number of poorly trained, inexperienced pilots also reacted against the increase of operational planes, and Dr. Tank estimated that twenty-five percent of aircraft wastage was caused by crashes on landings and other accidents, which could be attributed to pilot error.

#

The complete failure of the Luftwaffe to stop the allied landings on the Normandy beaches seems to have resulted from a combination of some of the factors discussed earlier in this chapter. According to the highest German sources, the Cotentin peninsula and the west bay of the Seine had long been suspected as possible landing areas for a cross-Channel invasion; complete surprise does not seem to have been achieved. Furthermore, enough planes to have offered a stiff defense appear to have been available. Why then was the GAF so completely helpless during the Normandy invasion?

For one thing, there was the shortage of experienced pilots as earlier referred. Transportation difficulties usually associated with the movement of the ground troops also caused trouble for the Luftwaffe. As the allied tactical air forces successfully interdicted the battle area from its hinterland, it became almost impossible to move short-range fighters into the area where they could reinforce the already greatly outnumbered Staffeln. The intensive bombardment of German-held air bases in northwest France also contributed to the impotency of the German fighter strength by making it very difficult for the GAF to operate in the battle area itself since most of the bases were ruined. Above all, there was not enough fuel to keep a large fighter force constantly in the air. Consequently, at the most critical moment of the war when the walls of Hitler's Festung Europa began to crack open, the vaunted German Air Force, the destroyer of Guernica, Warsaw, and Rotterdam, and Polish, Dutch, Russian, and French civilians beyond counting, was forced out of the air without a struggle.

For by the time the American and British soldiers were splashing through the Normandy surf and clambering up the beaches, victory over the Luftwaffe had already been won. The great air battles over Berlin, Schweinfurt, Wiener Neustadt, and Regensburg were all important landmarks along the road. But perhaps the greatest achievements were made far from the battle lines. The development of the long-range fighter, the indomitable flying qualities of the B-17, the tremendous build-up in little more than two years of four air forces operating against Europe were victories against the Nazis as important and far-reaching as those in the air. When the final and complete history of the war against the Luftwaffe is written, it will be a story of the combined skill of the pilot, bombardier, navigator, gunner, and ground crew united with the technician, the scientist, and the engineer, for it was by all of these men and women that the German air force was defeated.

A

APPENDIX: U.S. ARMY AIR FORCE COMBAT CHRONOLOGIES 1941-1945: D-DAY: THE BOMBER AND FIGHTER MISSIONS

6/6/44 Eighth AF Missions Flown

Heavy Bombers fly four missions in support of the invasion of Normandy. One thousand, three hundred and sixty-one HBs are dispatched on first mission of the day. One thousand and fifteen of the HBs attack the beach installations, forty-seven bomb transportation chokepoints in town of Caen, and twenty-one bomb alternate targets. Overcast and inability of HBs to locate (or absence of) Pathfinder leaders causes failure of some units to attack. The second mission strikes at transportation chokepoints in towns immediately around the assault area. Total cloud cover causes most of the 528 HBs dispatched to return with their bombs, but 37 bombers manage to bomb secondary target of Argentan. The third mission is dispatched against the important communication center of Caen. 56 B-24's bomb through overcast skies. Transportation chokepoints in towns immediately S and E of assault area are the objectives of the fourth mission for the Eighth. 553 HBs bomb tgts including Vire, Saint-Lo, Coutances, Falaise, Lisieux, Thury-Harcourt, Pont-l'Eveque, Argentan, and Conde-sur-Noireau. In all, 1,729 HBs of Eighth AF drop 3,596 tons of bombs during D-Day, suffering only 3 losses (to ground fire and a collision).

VIII Fighter Command has a threefold mission: escorting HBs, attacking any movement toward assault area, and protecting Allied shipping. The fighters fly 1,880 sorties including fighter-bomber attacks against 17 bridges, 10 marshalling yards, and a variety of other targets including convoy, railroad cars, siding, rail and highway junctions, tunnel, and a dam. Very little air opposition is encountered. The fighters claim twenty-eight German aircraft destroyed and fourteen damaged. Also destroyed are twenty-one locomotives and two carloads of ammunition. Numerous targets are damaged including locomotives, trucks, tank cars, armored vehicles, goods carriers, barges, and tugboats. Targets attacked with unreported results include warehouses, radar towers, barracks, troops, arty, staff cars, eighty-five trains, and a variety of other targets. 25 VIII FC aircraft are lost.

6/6/44 Ninth AF

More than 800 A-20's and B-26's bomb coastal defense batteries, rail and road junctions and bridges, and marshalling yards in support of the invasion forces landing in Normandy. Over 2,000 fighters fly sweeps, escort for MBs and TCs, ground support, and dive bombing missions over W France. During the preceding fight and during the day, over 1,400 C-47's, C-53's, and gliders deliver glider troops and paratroops, including 3 full airborne divisions, which are to secure beach exits to facilitate inland movement of seaborne assault troops. A total of about thirty airplanes—medium bombers, fighters, and transports—are lost.

6/6/44 Fifteenth AF

Shuttle-bombing (FRANTIC) continues as 104 B-17's and 42 P-51's (having flown to USSR from Italy on 2 Jun) attack A/F at Galati and return to Soviet shuttle bases. Eight enemy fighters are shot down and 2 P-51's are lost. Accompanied by figher escorts, 570-plus other HBs bomb oil refineries in Ploesti area, marshalling yards (M/Y) at Brasov and Pitesti, Brasov wagon and armament works, Turnu-Severin canal, and M/Y at Belgrade.

D+1
6/7/44 Eighth AF
AEAF directs air attacks against congested points to delay movement of more enemy forces into assault area. In the first mission, 402 HBs, including 20 Pathfinders, attack targets at Flers, Conde-sur- Noireau, Falaise, Argentan, L'Aigle, and Lisieux. Second mission is directed at Kerlin/Bastard A/F and at bridges, railroad junctions, depots, and station at Nantes, Angers, Tours, and adjacent areas. 498 HBs attack; heavy cloud prevents almost 100 others from bombing targets. VIII FC furnishes area spt for beachhead areas in early morning and to HB operations at midday and in late afternoon, at the same time maintaining harassment of comm and flying shipping patrol. The fighters encounter about 150 aircraft during the day, destroying 31. Enemy fighters account for four fighters lost. FB attacks are flown against about fifty targets, including M/Ys, sidings, trains, tunnels, bridges, convoys, A/Fs, and railroads. In almost 1,000 sorties, 25 fighters are lost.

6/7/44 Ninth AF
600-plus MBs hit bridges, junctions, trestles, coastal and field batteries, and M/Ys in France in support of invasion. Over 1,100 fighters support ground troops by dive bombing and strafing, escort MBs and transports, and make sweeps throughout the battle area as Bayeux is liberated and the Bayeux-Caen road is cut. 400-plus C-47's, C-53's, and gliders resupply para-troops in the assault area.

6/7/44 Fifteenth AF
340 B-17's and B-24's, some with ftr cover, hit Leghorn dock and harbor installations, Voltri shipyards, Savona railroad junction, and Vado Ligure M/Y, Antheor viaduct, and Var R bridge. 42 P-38's bomb Recco viaduct and 32 P-47's fly uneventful sweep over Ferrara-Bologna area.

6/8/44 Eighth AF
Attacks are made on comm to isolate German forward elements, and A/ Fs are bombed to prevent German air spt. Cloud conditions prevent over

400 HBs from executing assignments but 735 attack targets including A/Fs at Rennes and Le Mans and bridges, M/Ys and other railroad facilities, and various T/Os at or near Tours, Nantes, Cinq Marsla-Pile, Pontaubalt, La Vicomte-sur-Rance, Angers, Orleans, la Friliere, Etampes, and Morigny. 3 bombers are lost. VIII FC, flying 1,405 fighters sorties on this day, sends FB attacks against nearly seventy-five targets, including railroad facilities, bridges, convoys, A/Fs, barges, radio towers, troop concentration, a transformer, and a coastal gun. Fighters and fighter-bombers destroy nearly 400 rail, ground transport, and military vehicles and claim 46 airplanes destroyed. Twenty-two fighters of VIII FC are lost.

6/8/44 Ninth AF

Around 400 MBs attack rail and road bridges and junctions, rail sidings, M/Ys, town areas, fuel storage tanks, ammunition dumps, troop concentration and strong points in the Calais area. Around 1,300 fighters provide support to MBs and high cover over assault area, and bomb and strafe bridges, M/Ys, gun batteries,rail facilities, vehicles, towns, and troop concentrations.

Bad weather restricts operations to NW France. 873 HBs are airborne, but over 200 abort due to cloud conditions. Five hundred and eighty-nine HBs, including thirty-one Pathfinders, attack eight A/Fs in France and nine coastal installations in Pas de Calais area. One B-24 is downed by AA at Evreux. VIII FC, flying over 1,600 sorties, supports HB missions, launching attacks against about 80 targets, including railroad facilities, convoys, tank column, trucks, radar station, tunnels, gun emplacement, supply dump, and a power plant. About 225 vehicles, including train engines and cars, are destroyed, along with 16 enemy aircraft. Twenty-five fighters are lost.

6/10/44 Ninth AF

IX TAC establishes its first station on the Continent, at au Guay. Five hundred-plus B-26's and A-20's bomb targets in assault area in France. Targets include military concentrations, road and rail bridges and junctions, arty batteries, M/Ys, and town areas. Aircraft of more than fifteen ftr gps fly escort to bombers and transports, bombing numerous targets in support of ground assault, including rail facilities, roads, troop concentrations, arty, and town areas.

B

APPENDIX: THE US STRATEGIC BOMBING SURVEY, AIRCRAFT DIVISION INDUSTRY REPORT, SECOND EDITION JANUARY 1947, PREFACE AND SUMMARY CONCLUSIONS

Preface

1. In September 1944 the US Strategic Bombing Survey was organized under Presidential directive to conduct a survey of the effects of strategic bombing in hastening the German defeat. The American public is well aware that no small part of the cost of the European war can be charged to the Allied aerial offensive against strategic industrial installations. To them, an accounting must be given.

2. Strategic bombing is a highly scientific process. It is aimed at the systematic destruction of those resources that will most weaken the enemy by denying him the materials or weapons he needs to prosecute the war. Targets are selected only after a careful balancing of their significance to the enemy economy against the capabilities of the attacking force. To be successful, any strategic attack must cost the enemy many more man-hours lost than are expended in the attack.

3. During the war it was impossible to assess the real significance of this type of warfare. A limited amount of information on physical damage to industrial plants could be obtained from aerial photographs. Ground intelligence from agents inside Germany made an important contribution, and some German prisoners of war also told what they knew. It was impossible, however, to know with certainty whether or not the effects of air activity against the Reich justified the effort expended. The final accounting could only be made only after a careful on-the-spot investigation of the targets that had borne the brunt of the attack.

4. This report deals with the specialized but highly important part of the total strategic bombing effort - the attacks on the German aircraft and V-weapons industries. The destruction of this group of industries was considered of vital importance in support of the Allied air effort against Festung Europa. A number of key points in the industrial pattern were selected as objects of attacks. In this report an attempt is made to assess objectively the merits of the choice. It analyzes the German aircraft industry as it was before bombing and as it reacted to our attacks. Throughout the report, wherever the available data have permitted, comparisons are drawn between American and German production methods.

5. The report is based on field team investigation of a selected list of key targets in Germany, on interrogations of important German aircraft officials taken into custody after the collapse, and on analysis of government records of aircraft programs and production found hidden in caves, cellars and attics throughout Germany.

7. The report was prepared under the editorial leadership of Colonel Carl H. Norcross, formerly managing editor of Aviation Magazine. The group responsible for the preparation and the analysis of the German aircraft industry included: W. G. Friedrich, head of the Aeronautical Engineering Dept., North Carolina State College; N.W. Gilbert, Professor of Business Economics, California Institute of Technology; Jerome Lederer, Chief Engineer and Assistant Manager, Aero Insurance Underwriters; C.W. Miller, formerly Director, Planning and Airframe Supply, British Air Commission, Washington, D.C.; Myron A. Tracy, Acting Director, Aircraft Resources Control Office, Aircraft Production Board, Washington, D.C.;

and Stephen Zand, Director, Vese Memorial Aero Lab., Sperry Gyroscope Company.

Summary and Conclusions

1. This report deals with the effects of strategic bombing on the German aircraft industry.

2. Strategic bombing bears the same relationship to tactical bombing as does the cow to the pail of milk. To deny immediate aid and comfort to the enemy, tactical considerations dictate upsetting the bucket. To ensure eventual starvation, the strategic move is to kill the cow (with apologies to Mr Franklin D'Olier).

3. It is not always a simple matter to distinguish between strategic and tactical effort. For example, the heavy attacks against the German airframe assembly plants early in 1944 failed as a strategic effort because they produced only a mild indisposition in the great industrial "cow" that fed the Luftwaffe. "Bossy" refused to stay dead, and eventually succeeded in refilling the pail again and again. But in a tactical sense, the results were tremendously important. Hundreds of aircraft, which might otherwise have opposed Allied landings in Normandy, were left battered, twisting in the smoking ruins of Marienburg, Augsburg, Wiener Neustadt and Dessau. They were not available at the time the enemy needed them most.

4. Neither is it a simple matter to differentiate between the results of direct attack against strategic targets and indirect effects of attack against other segments of the enemy economy. Clearly, if all means of surface transport are wrecked to the point where deliveries of raw materials to factories for the manufacture of finished products become impossible, it is then of little consequence where the factories themselves are destroyed or remain intact. So if a complete electrical power failure could be brought about by bombing, what happens to plants dependent upon power to produce is only a question of academic interest.

5. To cut off the flow of usable aircraft to Hitler's fighting squadrons, the Combined Bomber Offensive applied every known form of attack. The Royal Air Force bombed cities and industrial areas by night to disrupt and demoralize labor and destroy such factories as might be located in the target area. The US Army Air Forces bombed airfields and factories by day to

destroy as many finished aircraft as possible and to cripple further production. At the same time, rail centers, bridges and marshalling yards were under constant attack by both air forces and tons of bombs rained down on oil refineries, synthetic fuel plants and fuel dumps. In the end, the total weight was too much, as Germany's industrial machine could not endure such punishment and finally collapsed.

6. How much each form of attack contributed to the end result is impossible to determine. Counting up the totals, however, and contrasting their potential capacity with actual accomplishment, it appears from this study that some 18,000 aircraft of all types were denied the German Air Force in the period of intensive attack between July 1943 and December 1944. (Reported production for the same period totaled 53,000 aircraft.)

7. Of the estimated production loss, roughly 78 percent or 14,000 aircraft were fighters. (Total reported fighter production for the period was 45,800.) Whether or not the German Air Force could have used all these additional aircraft effectively (because of shortages of fuel or of pilots), it is obvious the attacks against the German aircraft industry paid dividends. By keeping such a number of defensive fighters out of the air at times when the air war was critical, the job of wrecking Germany's manufacturing industries, her transportation system and cities was rendered that much easier, and the war was probably shortened by some months.

8. The question is still open, however, as to how many of those accomplishments resulted from the direct attacks against the aircraft industry. The records, which are presented in detail in this report, point up the tremendous recuperative powers of Germany's aircraft production. Paradoxically, aircraft production, appears, at first glance, to have been stimulated rather than retarded by the attacks. It must be remembered, however, that the great upswing in production that took place in the spring of 1944 had been planned and provided for during the six to nine months period preceding. How much higher the production curve would have risen had the attacks not been made is only a matter for conjecture. It was not until the fall of 1944, after the aircraft industry per se had ceased to be a primary target for the Combined Bomber Offensive, that production began to lag. Airframes, engines and parts were being manufactured in increasing numbers in the vast network of dispersed and concealed factories. But it was only after

transportation was disrupted and supplies of fuel dwindled that deliveries of finished aircraft to the GAF finally approached the vanishing point.

9. The quantitative study of the results of the strategic bombing of the German aircraft industry occupies the bulk of this report. Figure 1, which is not to be considered as a statistical presentation, is a composite picture of the trends of capacity, planning and production during the war years. The curves have all been "faired"; any quantitative vertical scale has been deliberately omitted. The relationship of the various elements of the chart, however, is in close agreement with the facts as disclosed in the detailed study that follows.

10. If strategic bombing did nothing but force the dispersal of the aircraft industry it would have paid its cost. The disruption to production occasioned by the physical movement of goods and machinery, the resulting loss of efficiency due to the dilution of management, the increasing load on an already overtaxed system of transportation were all factors in the final result. In the end, dispersal defeated itself, because once transportation systems failed, it became impossible to keep final assembly points fed with the necessary components parts and sub-assemblies to produce finished aircraft.

11. It was largely after that system failed that dispersal went into reverse. It was finally recognized that re-concentration of plants was necessary for efficient and economical operation. Concentrating plants above ground was obviously impossible. The only answer was to go underground. This decision came too late to be effective in the German war programs, but the cost of the effort added tremendously to the strain on the national economy. The millions of man-hours drained away from the available total to prepare such huge underground workings as those at Nordhausen and Neckar-Els may be credited directly to the account of strategic bombing.

12. Prior to the end of 1944 there is little evidence that lack of engines or of necessary equipment or of basic materials led to any critical shortages of finished aircraft. Even the widely publicized attacks against the ball bearing industry, which were supposed to pinch off a vital accessory to the building of aircraft and aircraft engines, failed to produce even as a temporary setback. The costly raid on Schweinfurt did cut heavily into ball bearing production. The stock bins and pipelines to airframe and aircraft engine plants, however, were so well-filled, redesign of equipment to eliminate ball bear-

ings progressed so rapidly, and the increased output of unbombed bearing plants was so great that the situation never became critical to the point of denying finished aircraft to the GAF.

13. It now appears that the most vulnerable points in the aircraft production pattern were not given the attention they deserved by target selection people or by operational groups. Apart from purely tactical considerations, attacks against the industry would have been more effective in the end had they been made further back in the manufacturing process rather than against final aircraft assembly points. Hindsight indicates that the aero-engine manufacturing plants were far more vulnerable than our intelligence might have been dealt with more profitably. For example, if shops housing fuselage assembly jigs could have been eliminated, if forge shops making crankshafts could have been put out of business, and if the manufacture of propeller blades could have been disrupted, the effects on final production would have been immediate and persistent. It was recognized only late in the war that certain foundries, which made certain highly complicated and specialized castings for jet engines, were the "Achilles heel" of the jet fighter complex. By taking out but a few such key shops, the production of the fighters on which Germany was depending to break up our long-range bombing attacks might have been seriously hampered.

14. Failure of British and American intelligence to disclose such vital targets was responsible in a larger measure for our failure to attack them. Through 1943, intelligence regarding German aircraft industry was reasonably good. After the industry dispersed, however, the quality of our intelligence deteriorated. We not only did not know the locations of many important units in the dispersal pattern, but we seriously underestimated the production capabilities and recuperability of the German industry. A high degree of optimism was injected into the estimates of production as a result of faulty interpretation of air-cover photographs and of reliance upon intelligence from unreliable sources. We underestimated almost by half the total aircraft production for 1944. Official estimated predicted a total of 22,440 aircraft; however, records show 39,807 machines were delivered to the German Air Force during that same period.

15. Physical damage studies point to the fact that machine tools and heavy manufacturing equipment of all kinds are very difficult to destroy or

damage beyond repair by bombing attacks. Buildings housing such equipment may be burned down and destroyed; however, after clearing away the wreckage, it has been found, more often than not, that heavy equipment, when buried under tons of debris, may be salvaged and put back into operation in a relatively short time and with comparatively little difficulty. Electrical equipment associated with heavy tools suffers most severely. A good fire in the vicinity of such equipment will destroy motors, control equipment and so forth. It has been generally observed, therefore, that incendiary attacks against airframe and aircraft engine parts are more effective than the equivalent amount of HE on the target.

16. There appears to have been some decline in the quality of German aircraft as a result of strategic bombing coupled with resultant dispersal. Certain items, possibly of superficial importance, were neglected as the pressure to produce went up. Little doubt exists that operations under dispersed and disrupted conditions presented unusual difficulties, but, throughout, inspection standards appear to have been generally well maintained. Above average losses in performance or losses of aircraft due to mechanical or other failures were undoubtedly experienced, but in the overall were relatively unimportant. One high ranking US Air Force officer has gone so far as to state that, except for their long range capabilities, we could have traded fighter aircraft with the Luftwaffe and still have beaten them in individual aerial combat. Our greatest advantage lay in the skill of our fighter pilots and not in any decisive technical superiority of equipment.

17. Looking at the picture as a whole, at the beginning of the war and as long as the initiative was theirs, German industrial planning was good. During the late 1930s, the aircraft industry had been built up to a point consistent with supposed military requirements. Early successes against untrained and under-equipped air forces, coupled with the fact that the losses in these early campaigns were far less than expected, developed a degree of overconfidence and resulted in pushing aircraft requirements well down the list of wartime priorities. Not until 1944, after the overall military situation had been reversed, were aircraft, particularly single-engine fighters, put back at the top of the priority schedule. By that time, however, a certain degree of desperation was in evidence, which eventually led to the deterioration of the aircraft industry and the GAF.

18. Hitler frequently interfered with the aircraft planning program because of his belief in the effectiveness of "secret" or "wonder weapons". Although no great percentage of the V-1 or the V-2 production was directly subtracted directly from the aircraft industry, Hitler's insistence on such weapons interfered seriously at times with material and labor supplies to the aircraft industry and caused dissension and disputes with respect to the relative importance of the two classes of weapons on the priority schedule.

19. All evidence concerning the later phase of the war points to a considerable amount of internal dissension, lack of coordination, and reliance on emergency measures to achieve results. One indication of this condition constantly comes to light during interrogation of topside personnel. Every one of them had engaged in a considerable amount of "buck passing" and was obviously making an effort to justify his own position and to prove that what happened to the German Air Force was not his particular fault.

20. During the period from 1941 to 1945, the relative position of German aviation planning and Allied aviation planning reversed itself. In the beginning, the planning for Germany's air effort was consistent and coordinated, while Great Britain and America were fumbling their way toward a plan and a program. From late 1943, however, German production planning became increasingly confused and muddled as Allied effort took shape and gained strength.

21. Strategic bombing of the German aircraft industry caused a direct and indirect loss of production amounting to approximately 18,000 airplanes between July 1943 and December 1944.

22. The best estimate that can be made distributes this loss of production about evenly between direct losses, caused by destruction of airframe plants, and indirect losses, caused by dispersal and inefficient operation under dispersal conditions.

23. If the German aircraft industry had not been dispersed, it is probable that an equal or even larger production loss would have been suffered.

24. The great rise in the number of airplanes turned out during the first half of 1944 was not so impressive when measured in terms of weight of airframe produced. In the end (1944) the overall efficiency of the German aircraft industry was less than fifty percent of that attained in the United States.

25. The German aircraft industry had at least a 100 percent excess capacity of plant and equipment before the Combined Bomber Offensive. This is indicated clearly by the fact that single-shift operation of most facilities was normal procedure prior to 1944.

26. The paradoxical increase in the rate of production following the heaviest attacks is explained by the fact that earlier planning programs were then on the point of producing maximum results. All pipelines were full and flowing. Also, because of the urgency of the situation, extraordinary expediting of shortages was carried out under the authority of the Speer Ministry, and political terrorism was occasionally resorted to through the Gestapo to increase output.

27. More attention should have been given earlier in the period of the Combined Bomber Offensive to attacks against aero-engine plants.

28. The quality of German aircraft tended to decline during 1944 because of the difficulties which attended dispersal operations, and because the inspection system began to operate less efficiently under high pressure. The extent of the decline in quality cannot be measured. It probably resulted in only a slight loss of performance for individual aircraft.

29. The alibis used by many German officials and industrialists blaming their failure to produce on a multiplicity of models, excessive program and engineering changes, can be discounted. Their situation in this regard was no more difficult than that which pertained in the United States.

30. The basic error made by Germany was probably Hitler's failure to increase the aircraft program at the time the Allies began the Combined Bomber Offensive. It is known that accurate information as to the plans and programs for building of aircraft in the United States was available to him, but he and Goering dismissed the figures as false and impossible, and thereby underestimated their eventual requirements to meet Allied attack.

31. The decision to abandon offensive action by long-range bombers against Allied industry and shipping, and to rely on the defensive capabilities of fighter aircraft proved also to be a strategic error of the first order. The chart gives a picture story of what happened to the German aircraft industry from the beginning of the war through to the final defeat. It is not a statistical presentation; rather, it is intended to give a qualitative picture of

the trends of capacity versus production, particularly during the period of expansion and attack.

Until early 1943 less than half the available capacity was utilized. The industry was coasting along on a one-shift per day basis. The big push for expansion began in 1943 when the High Command realized the potentialities of the Allied air attack: the realization came too late. The weight of attack that was delivered late in 1943 and early in 1944 set back production plans by many months, denying the German Air Force some thousands of aircraft at a time when it needed them most.

By the end of 1944 disintegration of the entire economy had set in. Transportation was disorganized to the point that essential materials could neither be delivered to the manufacturer, nor could finished products be taken away. Airframe assembly plants, though relatively invulnerable to direct attack due to dispersal and underground installations, could not get deliveries of engines, accessories, or sub-assemblies. Centralized planning broke down completely. Production of aircraft fell precipitously to a point far below the normal requirements of the GAF. By war's end, the manufacture of aircraft was at a standstill.